MORE MEMORIES OF
BURY

The publishers would like to thank the following companies for their

support in the production of this book

Main Sponsor

Halls

Abbeyfield Bury Society

Excelsior Group

Holy Cross College

Goergia Pacific GB Limited

Lepps Ltd

L Mortimer (Bury) Ltd

Newtons of Bury

Ernest Platt (Bury) Ltd

Printpack Limited

Radcliffe Glass & Windows Ltd

Slattery Patissier & Chocolatier

Wheeldon Brothers Waste Ltd

J&W Whewell Ltd

First published in Great Britain by True North Books Limited
England HX3 6AE
01422 344344

ISBN 1 903204 78 X

Text, design and origination by True North Books Limited
Printed and bound by The Amadeus Press Limited

MORE MEMORIES OF
BURY

Contents

Introduction

Welcome to 'More Memories of Bury'. This book is the latest in a series that revisits the town and its satellites that our parents and grandparents knew so well. Older readers will recall many of the forgotten scenes for themselves. Younger ones will be able to put in place the sights and sounds of 20th century Bury that they were told about with such affection. This new collection of delightful photographs brings back to life a time when the pace of life was so different. There really was an age when mobile phones did not disturb the peace of the lounge bar in the pub. Once upon a time we had individual and speciality shops and we can see some of them again inside this book. Supermarkets and shopping malls, ugly concrete office blocks and super fast highways were still to come when many of these images were captured and each one is accompanied by thoughtful captions. They contain a mixture of fact and reminiscence, all presented with one aim in mind, that of creating a mood of nostalgia for those days that are far behind us. The book makes no apology for indulging in that warm glow of reflecting on the past.

Times have changed, not always for the better, however not everything new is to be dismissed as a lowering of standards. 'More Memories of Bury' will also remind the reader of wartime days, when we feared the worst as bombers flew overhead on missions to Manchester, Salford and Liverpool. Those were the times when food, fuel and clothing were rationed and thousands went off to fight the enemy, never to return. There was the depression of the early 1930s and the austere times of postwar Britain when we had few electrical aids in our kitchens and housework was drudgery. We have left those days behind, but they are not forgotten. They have to be recalled to gain a balance when we celebrate the happier times.

This trip down memory lane will help bring to life those merrier occasions, made all the more poignant by recalling that it was not all sweetness and light. However, we can be forgiven for concentrating on the events, activities and sheer joie de vivre that has made Bury such a special place. This famous old Lancashire town became part of the new Greater Manchester County in 1974, following local government reorganisation. Nowadays it includes a

number of outlying towns and villages within its influence and boasts a population of around 180,000. This book concentrates on drawing upon photographs of when Bury was still as Lancashire as pigs' trotters, tripe, black puddings and flat caps. It looks at street scenes when Japanese, Korean, French and German cars were a rarity. Look carefully and you might be able to spot a Morris Cowley or Hillman Imp making its way along Silver Street.

The name Bury is derived from the Anglo-Saxon 'burg', or 'burh', meaning 'stronghold'. The area once covered in woodland, marsh and moor became a series of small settlements in the Bronze Age. There is also evidence that the Romans came to Bury in c78 AD and that Agricola built roads linking Chester, Manchester and Ribchester through Prestwich and Affetside. There are many who believe that Cockey Moor at Ainsworth is a corruption of 'Coccium', a Roman stronghold. Various artefacts, including coins, jewellery and pottery, have been unearthed that support the continued presence of the Latin invaders well into the 3rd century. Bury grew only gradually over the following centuries, but had established itself as a small market town by medieval times. The Lords of the Manor of Tottington, the De Montbegons, owned most of the land. This barony was granted to Roger de Poitou after the Norman Conquest of 1066 and, by the start of the 13th century, the manor was in the hands of Adam de Bury. It passed into the hands of the Pilkington family during the 14th century when Alice de Bury married Roger Pilkington. Sir Thomas Pilkington built Bury Castle, one of the most imposing Lancastrian buildings of the day, in 1469 on the site of a former Saxon manor. However, after the Pilkingtons backed the losing side in the Wars of the Roses, the lands were forfeited to the new king, Henry VII, who awarded them to one of his followers, Thomas, Lord Stanley. His elevation to the Earldom of Derby established a noble link with the Stanley family that continues today.

Much of the agriculture in the vicinity centred on the humble sheep, but it was this animal that provided the people with a major cottage industry of woollen making. Bury's burgeoning importance was confirmed when King Henry VI granted the town a royal charter in 1440 to hold a market. This was originally located in Market Place and, by the start of 18th century, was surrounded by a number of alehouses of which the Two Tubs is the sole survivor. Despite its

pride in its own identity, Bury was still a small town of only some 1,000 inhabitants, but that was soon to change. The woollen industry was superseded in economic importance by cotton in the 18th century. Both John Kay and his son Robert, inventors of the flying shuttle and drop box respectively, were 18th-century inhabitants of the district. John's invention of the 'picking peg' made the shuttle in a handloom move more quickly and the device revolutionised cotton weaving. When steam power was harnessed to drive machinery, the industrial revolution had arrived in Bury. In a 50 year period from the 1770s onwards, the population rose from 2,000 to 10,000. Although cotton was a major player, it was not the only industry. Papermaking was established and, by the end of the Victorian era, the town was the world's largest paper manufacturer. Transport had played its part in opening up markets across the country and, eventually, internationally. In 1791 the Manchester, Bolton and Bury Canal Company was formed and coal came to Bury by barge, with textiles and other goods making the return trip. The East Lancashire Railway opened on 1846, providing a link with Manchester and the outside world that meant even swifter passage of manufactured goods.

Bury continued to prosper as a thriving industrial centre into the last century, its numerous mill chimneys providing evidence of the nature of the main employment available. However, the decline in heavy industry after the second world war meant that Bury's working face was destined for change. It is to change that 'More Memories of Bury' is devoted. Buildings, social mores, language and lifestyles have all undergone alterations and, as the first pages are turned, this book will help readers relive the days when trams ran along Market Street, men stood up on buses to offer ladies their seats, shopkeepers sold cloth by the yard and not the metre and 'keep off the grass' was an instruction in a park and not one given to a university student. It is time to get into that wistful mood of thinking of the past when grandma was dancing the Black Bottom, dad was going off to pilot a Hurricane in the Battle of Britain or we were reading about Dan Dare in the Eagle. Why not suck on a Spangle or have a sip of dandelion and burdock from a stoppered bottle? Put Neil Sedaka's 'Oh Carol' onto the Dansette record player and let the waves of nostalgia start to flow.

Street Scenes

A royal visit always brought huge crowds out onto the streets because of our pride in the monarchy and the desire to see VIPs in the flesh. There was no television in 1921, so the only real images people really had of privileged figures came via photographs in newspapers. To have a visit from such high ranking personages as the Prince of Wales was a red letter day. Onlookers waved flags and called out words of encouragement and some men threw their hats into the air. As the motorcade swept the future Edward VIII into town and along Market Street, people cheered as much for the monarchy as for the young prince himself. In 1917 his father, George V, took the popular measure of abandoning the Germanic name of Saxe-Coburg-Gotha and replacing it with Windsor, giving the royal family an authentically British sound. The heir to the throne was on his way to take lunch with Lord Derby and other dignitaries in Derby Hall, the building on the left designed by Sidney Smirke that opened in 1850. Later joined by the Derby Hotel and Athenaeum, this formed an integrated complex all the way down to where Kay Gardens can be found. The Tea and Coffee Rooms on the opposite corner had some decorations and banners attached to the exterior, but such displays of loyalty were relatively limited as Prince Edward had asked for prudence in expenditure in difficult times.

Below: Fleet Street, later to be known as The Rock, was blessed in September 1933 with a variety of architectural styles. Better that than the rectangular uniformity that blighted the minds of designers in the 1960s and 1970s who could only think in straight lines. The street had a quaint sense of individuality in the interwar years. Calderbank was later to become a small Boot's outlet before the two storey replacement was built. The Maypole Dairy was a delightful place to be self indulgent, among the delicious, mouthwatering, creamy products on sale. Burton's was, perhaps, the most imposing edifice on the block. The majority of the men's tailoring stores that Montague Burton had built conformed to this style, with its columns and light coloured brickwork. Before the days of boutiques, unisex and casual wear, men's tailoring was big business. Even small towns could support Burton's, John Collier, Weaver to Wearer, Dunn's, Alexandre, Hepworth's and the Fifty Shilling Tailor all trading profitably. Burton's chain of stores advanced rapidly from humble beginnings at the start of the last century. He acquired a huge factory in Leeds in 1925, employing 10,000 workers and was said to opening a new shop every month in the 20s and 30s. By World War II he was clothing a quarter of the male population. Both Boot's and Burton's moved to new sites in the Mill Gate Centre in the 1970s.

Above: The snack bar is on Spring Street at the corner of George Street and the father and child are heading towards what is now Angouleme Way, at the southern end of the car park for Angouleme Retail Park. As dad crosses the cobbled street, trousers flapping in the breeze, he shows all the love and affection a man can have for his son. He hopes and dreams that life will deal him a better hand than the one he was given, being brought up in a back to back without hot water on tap and having to make do with bread and jam for tea because his own father was struggling to find regular employment in the depression years. By 1955, with rationing and privation largely behind him, this father knew that jobs were more plentiful and that a mood of optimism was returning to the country. With a new degree of confidence in the air, he could start to enjoy being a dad. There were Dinky cars in the shops for them to play with together. He might even be able to run to a Hornby electric train set now that he was on piecework. Perhaps the lad had a future in engineering. If so, then a Meccano set or steam engine fuelled by methylated spirit would be perfect. Where is this little fellow now, for he will be in his 50s with fond memories of the man who lifted him over the turnstile at Gigg Lane, wiped his eyes when he fell off his first two wheeler and bought him his first half when he was still a couple of years shy of being 18, Dads and lads, inseparable.

The Rock, or Fleet Street as it still was in 1930, had shops that were locally owned and run competing for business next to those that were part of developing chains. Boot's dispensing chemist is a name we all know, but even the great and good have humble beginnings. Jesse Boot, later Lord Trent, opened the first of his many shops in Nottingham in 1877. His father had an interest in country potions and remedies that Jesse inherited. He experimented with all manner of combinations of herbs that he turned into patent medicines. Boots' shops, though, concentrated on more established lines as Jesse opened other stores in Lincoln, Sheffield and Derby. He became well loved for his charity work, giving away much of his fortune. He died a year after this photograph was taken. The shop next door, at 29 Fleet Street, bears one of the nicknames given to Montague Burton, being known as the 'Thirty shilling tailor' in some towns before having his own name on every store. The title was used in competition with Leeds' Henry Price (1877-1963), the 'Fifty shilling tailor' men's outfitter. Price acknowledged that, despite money being tight in the interwar years, men still wanted to dress as elegantly as they could afford and he spotted a niche in the market, establishing his chain, selling cheap, but acceptable, clothing. Soon he had a chain of stores across the country that remained popular throughout the 1950s until greater prosperity and a desire for more fashionable clothing altered purchasing patterns. Price was knighted in 1937 and, after his passing, left a legacy of fond memories of the days when his suits cost just £2.50, in today's terminology.

Above: The tram was one of many football specials taking fans to Gigg Lane to watch the Shakers in action. Large crowds followed the team that had a tremendous legacy as one of the clubs playing in the first days of the Football League. Bury won the FA Cup twice at the early 1900s, with a 6-0 thrashing of Derby still standing as the record score and winning margin in a final. As the fans got on board, notice how few women there were c1930 with an interest in the national game. It is almost certain that this photograph was taken on a Saturday, long before the god called Sky moved in to decide when and where games were played. The establishment on the extreme left corner belonged to the Bury Coffee House and Refreshment Company, formed in 1878. The tram could trace its roots back to the Tramways Company that began service in March 1883 from here to Blackford Bridge and beyond. Electrification arrived in June 1903 on the Moorside to Jericho section and by 1907 had reached Heap Bridge, Whitefield, Tottington and Radcliffe. The various routes were all cabled by 1915. The Corporation decided to pull the plug from the trams in the1930s, but abandonment of the tramways was delayed because of the war. The last one ran on the Walmersley section in February 1949.

Below: This float was receiving some finishing touches to its decorations as the No 29 tram eased its way past. The Crown Brewing Company Limited changed its name from the Bury Co-operative Brewing Distilling Company Limited in 1866 and before long had established its Crown Ales as one of the more popular tipples to go down the throats of local drinkers. At its peak, the brewery owned 140 licensed houses and a large works on Rochdale Road. The company was taken over by Dutton's of Blackburn in 1959 before becoming part of the Whitbread empire. Unfortunately, as CAMRA members will testify, individual breweries with their specially formulated beers have been disappearing all too often during the latter years of the last century. The big boys swallowed many of them up, but common sense and profit have made some of them think again. There is a market for distinctive ales, as seen in such shining examples as Black Sheep of Masham, a spin off when the Theakston brewery was gobbled up. In recent years, the smaller names have made a comeback. Jennings of Cumbria has relaunched Ward's of Sheffield and John Smith's rescued Barnsley's original yeast culture from the National Yeast Bank and recommenced brewing Barnsley Bitter in 1994. The Crown Ales float was part of the 1926 celebrations either for the jubilee pageant or Manchester Civic Week.

Right: The buildings in this part of Bury largely date from mid Victorian times. The White Lion on Bolton Street was built in 1880, some 10 years after its neighbour on the corner of Market Place. Lloyds Bank, now Wylde's Bar, was formerly home to Driffield's outfitters and drapers and where, at the rear of the property in the former entrance to the old stable yards, the Ribble Bus Company once had a booking office. Even earlier, the Manchester, Bury, Rochdale and Oldham Steam Tramway Company also had offices here in Victorian times. We can see from this 1953 photograph that traffic was light, despite the road being part of the main route through town from Rochdale to Bolton. This was the year of the Coronation and the nation hoped that the crowning of a new queen would bring as much prosperity as Britain had seen the last time it had a woman on the throne. Her subjects felt that surely the austere days of postwar Britain would soon have to come to an end. It was nearly eight years since the last shot was fired and, yet, we still had ration books for some items. There had been two changes of government, but we still struggled to throw off the feeling that there were other countries that had fared better from being on the winning side.

Bottom left: In the 1920s a person could walk from Moorgate to Market Square along this stretch of road and discover that the name changed three times as four titles were used along the way. As with many bureaucratic decisions, it took an inordinate amount of time before a conclusion was reached. Many officials liked 'Fleet Street', one of the names already in use, but others favoured 'High Street' or something with 'Avenue' in it. Fortunately, common sense prevailed and the Council took notice of the general public, for a change. Locals had generally used 'The Rock' as a description for the whole street, so the elected members bowed to the inevitable, though it took them 12 years to concede the point officially. Looking along The Rock in 1954, we are facing away from Union Street behind the camera and gazing towards Moorgate in the far distance. Well beyond the junction with Rochdale Road on the right, a little period piece is parked by the left hand roadside. The Morris Traveller, with its timber framed coachwork, was a delightful icon of that era and has become something of a collector's item. The steel framed Hornby Buildings, near right at 118-126 The Rock, were built in 1933 by Bury Corporation and were named after a former landowner. The date is in relief on the terracotta façade.

Below: Many of the properties on Bolton Street, within a few hundred yards of Market Place, have changed little over the last 50 years. Further down the road it is all different now that Jubilee Way sweeps traffic to the west of town on its way from Manchester to Bolton. But this little section of town still appears as if life has passed it by. A lot of the property looked drab in 1958 and in the new millennium is all but the same, as if trapped in a time warp. The businesses may have changed, but little else has happened to disturb the Rip van Winkle existence of Bolton Street. Soccer lovers will know that this was the year of the Munich disaster when eight Manchester United players, along with a number of officials and journalists, perished in a plane crash. Supporters at Gigg Lane bowed their heads in silent tribute at the next home match. Elsewhere, there were jollier scenes when West Indian Garfield Sobers, the former Radcliffe professional, broke Len Hutton's Test record by compiling a masterly 365 not out against Pakistan. There were mixed emotions when neighbouring Bolton Wanderers lifted the FA Cup, beating a depleted Manchester United with the help of a Nat Lofthouse double. Over in Sweden, Brazil won the World Cup with the help of a teenager called Pele. Some said he was a flash in the pan, but did not like to be reminded of that in the years to come.

This delightful view across Kay Gardens was taken in 1954. Built on the site of the Earl of Derby's 1839 indoor market, it includes the domed memorial to John Kay (1704-64). This site lay derelict after a new market opened in 1901, but in 1903 it was agreed to lay out the gardens in memory of the man who brought the world the flying shuttle. Henry Whitehead, a local benefactor thought to have been one of Kay's descendants, paid for the monument that was erected in 1908. John Kay's invention helped to revolutionise textile production, but brought him little in the way of fortune or happiness. Woollen manufacturers in Yorkshire were quick to adopt his idea, but they organized a protective club to avoid paying Kay a royalty. The Tykes have always had a reputation for being tight. Not only did he lose most of his money in litigation to protect his patent, but he was also subjected to violent threats from handloom weavers whose livelihood was threatened by mechanisation. Kay and his family moved to France where he is said to have died in obscurity. Market Street is to the right of the gardens, leading away towards the spire of the parish church on the edge of Market Place. The two buses passing one another are on Haymarket Street, to the left of the junction with Broad Street.

usy, busy, busy was how it was on The Rock in 1950 as these shoppers put their best feet forward and marched briskly towards whatever destinations they had in mind. The mums pushed their babies in prams that did good service, often being passed around family members whenever another little cousin came along. Mums looked after their offspring and lavished them with all the care and attention that they needed. They took the advice of their own mothers and made sure that little Norman and Sheila got their jabs on time, were bathed in water carefully elbow tested and wrapped in nappies that were carefully boiled clean. They also read stories to them and played games with them as they grew into toddlers. There was no suggestion that the little ones should be farmed out to a childminder or abandoned in some nursery because, in 1950, we looked after our own. Any help that might be needed was provided by a neighbour or one of our relatives who lived just a block or two away. The advert for 'quality cycles' might make some readers think of one of Bury's famous sons. It was a common put down in the 1950s to say to some cyclist who was going too fast, 'Who do you think you are, Reg Harris?' Born in 1929, he was one of the all time great names in international cycling. He won two silver medals in the 1948 London Olympics before becoming the World Amateur Sprint Champion in 1949, 1950, 1951, 1952 and 1954. He died in Macclesfield in June 1992, after collapsing while still riding his bike at the age of 72! A memorial statue to his memory stands in the Manchester Velodrome.

Above: Even though the motorcar in the picture gleamed like a new pin, its style was utterly dated. The front door opened 'the wrong way' and the tiny sidelights perched on the wings gave the vehicle an antiquated look. The condition of James Clegg's Bargain Store and the gas streetlamp nearby also hinted at a need for modernisation. This was in 1952 and parts of our town, in keeping with the rest of the country, were suffering from the legacy of the war. Money and effort, not surprisingly, had been ploughed into the effort of freeing ourselves from the threat of the Nazi jackboot. But, in so doing we had all but bankrupted ourselves. Investment in housing, industry and transport had been almost non-existent since before the war. The Americans' Marshall Plan, more properly called the European Recovery Programme, in part bailed us out. The USA launched a scheme to help Europe get back on its feet, though Uncle Sam's motives were drawn as much from fear of Reds under the bed as they were from kindness. President Truman believed that the poverty, unemployment and dislocation of the postwar period were reinforcing the appeal of communist parties to voters in western Europe. Even though American aid started to ease our burdens, it took a long time to complete the regeneration of Britain. Run down parts of town like this stayed with us for quite some time.

Bottom: In 1951 the photographer was looking along this row of shops on the right hand side of the A58 Rochdale Road, facing towards the start of The Rock and where the roundabout with Angouleme Way would be created. Heaton's, on the corner of York Street, was the mid 20th century version of unisex hairdressing. However, unlike he modern variety, the sexes were segregated once through the door. Women sat under the dryer for ages getting those waves permanent, or as close to it as could be arranged. Men arranged to have their short back and sides, topped with a dab of Brylcreem a la Denis Compton, an hour or so after their wives arrived. Alternatively, they came with them and nipped out for a Crown's Ale or two before returning for the missus. We were a lot more trusting over 50 years ago. The bicycle propped up against the window would still be there when its owner stepped out of the barber's chair, neck tingling from the close cut and clutching 'something for the weekend'. Imagine leaving anything unattended for more than a moment in the current climate. No cyclist goes out these days without a substantial chain and padlock, making sure that his machine is well secured before he leaves it. He would not be surprised to find that the bike was still there on his return, but that someone had pinched the lamppost.

Above: The advert for Capstan cigarettes on the hoarding on Tithebarn Street will mean something to heavy smokers. A full strength Capstan before breakfast was the best way to start the day with a spinning head and the need for a sit down before falling over. Goodness, they packed a punch. In 1958, as we look along The Rock, lovers of the dreaded weed will recall that most men smoked untipped cigarettes. Those with a lump of cork on the end were for women and softies. But, you had to be careful when taking one out of your mouth as any sudden action brought a piece of skin from your lip attached to the fag end. Either that or it stuck in the lips as the inside of the middle and index fingers slid down the tube, suffering a nasty burn. Oh, the joys of smoking! Tithebarn Street, as the name suggests, once boasted such a 17th century building. Tithe is the old English for a tenth and has its origins in the church, but the practice of contributing that fraction of a person's income for religious purposes goes back to the Old Testament. It was adopted by Christianity as a means of providing an income for the clergy and maintenance for the churches. Farming communities often contributed produce or stock instead of money. Some landowners adopted the church's practice and used tithes as a means of collecting rent.

Top right: Sir Robert Peel has looked down upon Market Place, with The Rock to the left, since 1852 when the £2,500, 12 foot high statue was erected to honour one of Bury's most famous sons. The monument was unveiled in his memory by Frederick Peel MP, two years after the death of the man who inspired the name 'bobby' for a policeman was killed in a riding accident. Robert Peel (1788-1850) was born at Chamber Hall, the eldest son of a wealthy cotton manufacturer, Robert Peel (1750-1830), who was made a baronet by William Pitt the Younger. The younger Robert was educated at Harrow and Oxford and, with his father's money, a parliamentary seat was found for him as soon as he came of age. Peel became Home Secretary in 1822 and, during his term of office, created the Metropolitan Police force. He served two terms of office as prime minister (1834-35 and 1841-46) and is particularly remembered for repealing the Corn Laws and his liberalism in attitude towards Catholic emancipation. Neither of these endeared him to landowners or die-hard Protestants. Peel was a proud, shy person, by nature quick-tempered, but courageous and stubborn in his sense of purpose. The 128 foot Peel Tower on Holcombe Hill was erected on Thursday, 9 September 1852, the day after his statue was unveiled in Market Place. This photograph dates from July 1963.

Right: Sam Taylor's toys and sports shop on Silver Street in 1958 was full of gems that kept youngsters happy for hours. Many a dad could be seen looking in the window, secretly longing to buy a goods engine for his own enjoyment rather than his son's electric train set. There was a definite air of sexism about in those days when it came to selecting children's toys. Girls had their dolls' houses, nurses' uniforms and needlecraft kits, whereas boys got Subbuteo soccer, cap guns and Airfix kits. Although girls could cross over the great

gender divide and play with racing cars or indulge in model making, lads simply dare not push a toy pram or indulge themselves in the dressing up box. A lass climbing a tree was a tomboy, but a boy holding a rag doll was a sissy. The Bury District and Co-operative Society building belonged to a part of the movement that first saw light of day just a few miles down the road in Toad Lane, Rochdale. In 1844 a group of traders pooled their meagre resources in a self help measure that was also intended to benefit customers. They were able to buy more cheaply in greater bulk and could pass on the savings to the general public who became part of the organisation as it received a dividend, fondly called 'divvy', earned by the sum of its purchases. More properly called the Rochdale Equitable Society of Pioneers, the co-operative movement's ideas and ethics soon spread across the northwest and, ultimately, nationally and internationally.

Right: In the distance the mill chimneys still dominated the skyline in the early 1960s, belching out their smoke as they had done since the heady days of the industrial revolution. The distinctive dome of the old market and the white façade of the Bury District Co-operative Society building on Haymarket Street stand out clearly. The domed monument in Kay Gardens is just visible to the left. The abattoir on Knowsley Street is the focal point of the foreground. It opened in 1903 and cattle were brought in by truck and rail from special sidings at Knowsley Street Station. The actual slaughterhouse was at the rear of the building, perhaps a case of out of sight out of mind. Even the strongest of stomachs turns a little at the thought of the fate awaiting those poor beasts making their final journey before being turned into Sunday roasts. Some of the smells drifting out from the abattoir were memorable, to say the least. The commercial side of the business was not very successful, but the opening of the Town Hall opposite in 1954 accelerated its demise. It closed in 1972 and the site cleared for a car park. The two ornamental lions on the gable were preserved and moved to Bury Lions' Garden in Crompton Street, where they still can be seen in the remodelled Lion Square.

Bottom: The trees in the churchyard outside St Mary's spread their branches across Market Place as the lady cyclist bowled along the road in 1964. Just beyond the leafy arbour, the building peeking out on the left dates from 1874. With the address of 1 The Rock, it marks the transition from one part of town to another. Known as the Union Buildings, it has a mock Tudor façade somewhat out of keeping with the solid stone of others of a similar age. In the distance, the imposing store built for Downham's ironmongery business, founded in 1853, is at the head of this part of The Rock on the corner with Union Street. The company merged with John Kay and Sons two years before the store was demolished in 1971 to make way for further pedestrianisation. Stationery Box and Mothercare now occupy more modest premises on this site. Just nearer the camera, on this side of Union Street, we can see William Deacon's Bank, now the Royal Bank of Scotland. The lower building, next up, is now the NatWest. Entrance to the section of The Rock that continues beyond Downham's is now closed to traffic. The street only took the name we now know it by in 1935 when it was decided to rename the whole length of road from St Mary's Church to Moorgate. It had formerly been split into Fleet Street, Rock Street, Stanley Street and Water Street.

This little lad, in his regulation short trousers and rumpled socks, looks to be riding a bike that is a good size too big for him. The seat and handlebars are about as low as they can go, so it is something of a surprise that the man on the pavement has not picked up on it. He was one of the officials overseeing the cycling proficiency test in Radcliffe in 1950. Children followed a series of lessons and lectures on safe cycling and practised what they had learned on mock up streets, equipped with little traffic lights and T junction signs, chalked onto the playground at school. They brought their cycles at weekends or in the evenings and learned how to mend a puncture, inflate their tyres and keep the lights in good order. Having digested the contents of the Highway Code, they were sent out onto the road to be tested on their knowledge and application of safe cycling. The cenotaph in the background is at the junction of Spring Lane and Blackburn Street. Unveiled on 25 November 1922, it is inscribed with the names of 641 local men who lost their lives in World War I. There was a further ceremony on 30 April 1949 when another 150 sad entries from World War II were made on four extra plaques.

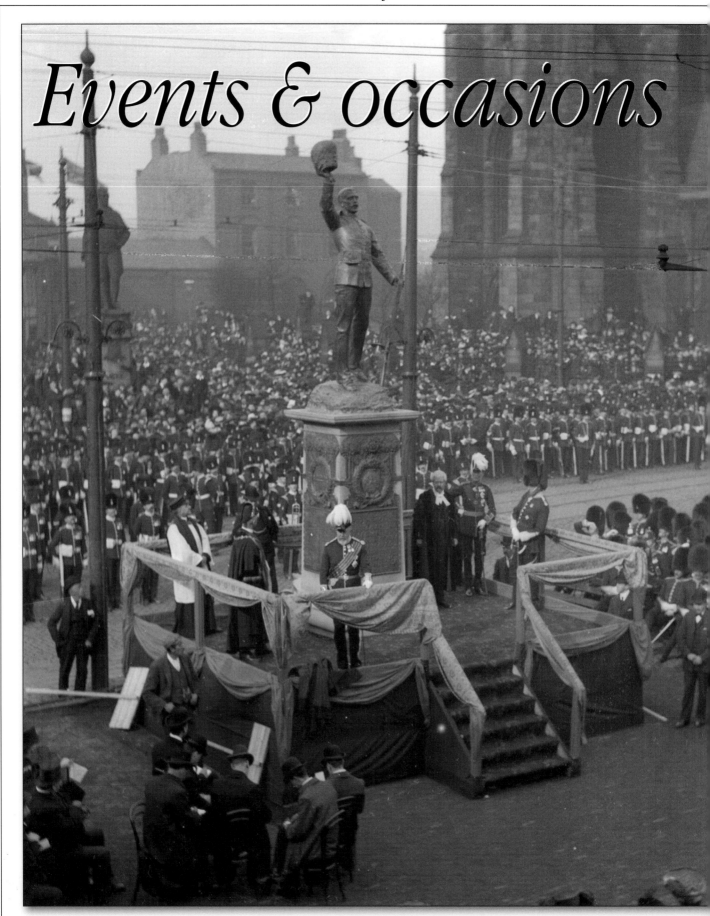

Events & occasions

Left: George Frampton (1860-1928) is a famous name in architectural circles. Knighted in 1908, his major work was in sculpting statues, with ones to Queen Victoria in Leeds, Peter Pan in Kensington Gardens and Edith Cavell in St. Martin's Lane, London being among the most memorable. On Saturday, 18 March 1905, Lord Derby, in the uniform of the Lord Lieutenant and accompanied by Mayor, Alderman Butcher, unveiled Frampton's Boer War memorial in Market Place. Rather than a display of grief for the fallen, the military figure on top of the monument displayed an urgency for battle. After the ceremony, the Lancashire Fusiliers made the short march to the Drill Hall where tea was served to a party of old folks. This regiment fought at Spion Kop in the South African campaign, but their honours come from many more wars than the one fought in 1899-1902. One particularly notable victory occurred at Minden in the Seven Years' War when the French were put to flight. A decade after the unveiling of the memorial, the Fusiliers were to have one of their finest, but saddest, hours when many lost their lives at Gallipoli. The heroism of Willis, Bromley, Grimshaw, Keneally, Richards and Stubbs won them fame as the six who won Victoria Crosses before breakfast on that awful day in 1915. The Boer War memorial can now be found in Whitehead Gardens on Knowsley Street.

Below: The Prince of Wales arrived in Bury in an open topped Rolls Royce as an aeroplane thrilled the crowd by looping the loop overhead. On 6 July 1921 he shook the hands of veterans of the first world war. As can be seen from the condition of the next but one to be greeted, not everyone had recovered from his battle wounds nearly three years after the armistice had been signed. Many old soldiers had permanent scars or missing limbs, while others were blind or suffering the long term effects of mustard and chlorine gas poisoning. Then there were those who look outwardly unscathed, but suffered nightmares and depression for years to come, brought on by the horrors they witnessed at close quarters. The bowler hatted Prince Edward, Albert, Christian, George, Andrew, Patrick, David, to give him his full mouthful, was the 27 year old future king who would throw the country into crisis with his abdication in 1936. He had both a naval and army background. Although trained (1907-11) for the Royal Navy, he was commissioned in the Army's Grenadier Guards after the outbreak of World War I and served as a staff officer. As heir to the throne he was not permitted to serve in the front line, but at least he could converse with these men with some first hand knowledge of military matters.

Bottom: There was hardly a square inch of ground to be seen in Union Square during this gathering c1939. The reason for bringing together such a multitude might not be immediately apparent. From the approximate date, some might presume that it is an assembly listening to some pronouncement about the outbreak of war. Others might guess at a gaggle of racegoers or football supporters waiting to be whisked off to some sporting venue. But, the answer to the conundrum can be found by looking carefully above the people's heads. There are several banners being waved and these belonged to various churches and religious groups. Union Square dates back to July 1784 when Richard Howarth, a printer, laid down the corner stone of the first building. From then it became a frequent gathering spot on important occasions. It became established as the focal point for the Whit walks. In the first half of the last century we were great church attenders and supported displays that advertised our beliefs. Even for those who were not devout Christians, Whitsuntide was a time to come into Union Square and indulge in some community hymn singing. Strains of 'I vow to thee my country' or 'Abide with me' drifted across the heads of those taking part in the walks and local brass bands happily included religious music within their repertoires. In Bury, the devil definitely did not have all the best tunes.

Right: The interwar years were definitely those of the flat cap. Perhaps in another 80 years a future generation will look back at the 1990s and 2000s as the days of the baseball cap, though it is doubtful that the present headgear fad will generate similar nostalgia. Other than the altar boys, nearly everyone in this photograph wore something on his or her head, whether it be cloche hat, helmet, homburg or the symbol of the working classes. This parade, part of the annual Whit walks, approached the scaffolded building of the reconstructed fire station due to be officially opened about four months later on 7 October 1925. The procession was moving along Stanley Street, the part of Bury that came under the general name of The Rock 10 years later. Heap Bridge Band accompanied the large number of church congregations that demonstrated their particular allegiance. The Anglican walk took place on Whit Friday, with the Catholic procession occurring on the Sunday. The former headed for the parish church of St Mary, while the latter went just a little further onto Manchester Road where St Marie's RC Church is situated. The Catholic walk was often led by a priest or an acolyte swinging a thurible in which incense was burning, casting a distinctive smell across the watching crowd.

Top right: The Whit walk was an annual event until the 1960s when the Spring Bank Holiday was created as a public holiday. Many churchgoers were horrified that a state holiday could replace a religious festival. Non-denominational traditional-ists were not best pleased either and saw the decision as the erosion of yet another bit of English culture. As well as a profession of faith, these walks used to be an occasion when children showed off their new clothes, specially bought for all to see. Youngsters had to take good care of them because there was trouble in store if they came home with a snagged dress or torn

trousers. They were special occasion clothes and
definitely not for messing about in or getting up to
some sort of tomfoolery. After the procession and
service in church, children went off to visit aunts
and uncles they might not have seen since the
previous year. It was the custom to give the kids a
small present of money when they came to call.
The shilling or florin was carefully put away and
deposited in a moneybox shaped like a pig or a
telephone box and raided for spending money
when the Wakes Weeks came along. Most adults
were pleased to see their nephews and nieces, but
there was always the odd grumpy uncle about.
When the children came knocking, he was known
to call out to his wife, 'Your sister Ada's kids are
here. It must be Whit Sunday because they have
got their hands out.'

Above: In May 1930 the Guild of St Agnes came along The Rock and turned the corner at Market Place, close to the former Derby Hotel that once stood next to Derby Hall on Market Street. The dainty young girls holding the banner strings represented purity and innocence, this guild's mantra. It is dedicated to the memory of the 4th century Roman, the patron saint of girls. The 13 year old Agnes dedicated herself to Christ and, when a youth who attempted to violate her was struck blind, she healed him with prayer. The procession was on its way to the handsome St Marie's Church, built in 1841 for the large numbers of Irish immigrants who came here to work on canal and railway construction. Those escaping the potato famine swelled their numbers later in that decade. The custom of holding Whit walks began in the early 19th century when Anglicans paraded around St Ann's Square, Manchester. Catholics did not adopt the custom until

after World War I. This procession had just passed the church of St Mary the Virgin that stands on a Bronze Age burial site. There was a place of worship here in the late 12th century and considerable rebuilding occurred in 1776, with more to come in the 1870s. The spire dates from 1845. The war memorial to the left was erected in 1924 and unveiled on Armistice Day by the mother of George Stanley Peachment, a posthumous holder of the Victoria Cross.

Bottom left: Heading along The Rock in 1930, this Whit walk procession moved along the cobbled roadway following some of the tram tracks that served the town for most of the first half of the last century. A steam tramway first left Market Place for Whitefield and Prestwich on 12 March 1883, but the heydays of this nostalgic form of transport began with electrification in 1903 and a journey from Moorgate to Jericho. The red and white trams stopped running after a journey to Walmersley on 13 February 1949. The day chosen for this parade along the tracks could hardly have been worse. The setts were slippery and bandsmen's fingers chilly as the cold rain coursed down. Looking carefully at the foreground it seems that one musician has lost a drumstick, but no doubt he was able to improvise. The foul weather does not appear to have dampened the enthusiasm of the onlookers as they shelter under a forest of umbrellas. Those who arrived early got the best view and a seat to go with it. It was a shame that carefully prepared

costumes and fine garlands were wringing wet, but none of this deterred the marchers from enjoying the occasion. Catholics and Protestants held their processions on different days, but there was never any trouble when they took place. What a contrast with Belfast when the Orangemen or Nationalists hold their parades and it becomes open season on those with opposing backgrounds. Bury folk just enjoyed each other's processions as spectacles.

Above: Wellington Playing Fields played host to this children's pageant that was part of the 1926 golden jubilee celebrations. Bury received its charter of incorporation in September 1876 and marked the 50th anniversary with parades and pageants. One of the largest and most picturesque was that organised by Mr W Morgan, a physical education instructor. The band of the 5th Battalion of Lancashire Fusiliers played as 15 special trams shipped 7,000 children to the fields. Watched by a huge crowd of parents and friends, the youngsters assembled to create the image of the town coat of arms. Each part of the insignia has a special meaning and includes elements from Tottington, Radcliffe, Ramsbottom, Whitefield and Prestwich in addition to Bury itself. The top sections display an anvil and a fleece, with the bottom pair having two crossed shuttles and two papyrus haulms or culms. The Mayor, Councillor Hartley rounded off the proceedings with the announcement that the children were to have an extra day's holiday from school in honour of the special day and the effort they had shown. Teachers smiled in appreciation as parents groaned. Bury became a county borough in 1888 and was brought into Greater Manchester in 1974 after the reorganisation of local government. Most locals still regard this as a nonsense, firmly believing that they are Lancastrians and not Mancunians.

Below: The day dawned damp and murky, but no-one on Norman Street, now itself part of history, seemed to have a care in the world. This was the day that Queen Elizabeth II was being crowned in Westminster Abbey and 2 June 1953 was going to become a part of folklore. Bunting bedecked the street and Union flags hung from windows and telegraph poles. We might have lived in humble surroundings, but we knew how to party and there were festivities the like of which we had not seen since VJ Day in 1945. Down in London crowds turned out in the rain and watched the coronation procession of foreign royals and dignitaries go past. One of the most endearing memories is of a beaming Salote, Queen of Tonga, waving to everyone from an open topped carriage that was gradually filling with rain. On Norman Street, the residents tucked into butties and buns and the children played street games of musical chairs on ones dragged out from kitchens. An old wind-up gramophone played 'She wears red feathers' by Guy Mitchell and all the little ones joined in with Lita Roza's 'How much is that doggie in the window?' Rumour had it that someone round the corner had a television set and was watching the ceremony being described by Richard Dimbleby. Now, there was posh.

Above: Flags and bunting were festooning the whole of Bury in 1926, but perhaps nowhere as significantly as at 26 Silver Street. The garlands and streamers, perhaps some left over from celebrations after the Great War, were hung in Bury's own honour. This was the 50th anniversary of achieving borough status and the occasion was marked with a mixture of dry, public speaking and general merriment. The municipal offices and council chamber occupied the upper floors, though the ground floor was used for banking purposes. The building was erected in 1867 for the Bury Banking Company that amalgamated with the Lancashire and Yorkshire Bank in 1888. In 1928 it continued to serve the financial world when Martin's Bank moved in and that form of business was continued when Barclays swallowed up Martin's in the late 1960s. That latter banking giant still retains the premises, though the seat of local government has been at the new Town Hall, in between Manchester Road and Knowsley Street, since 1954. The town council should have used Derby Hall as a base, but a spat with Lord Derby meant that the elected members refused to meet there, though a magistrates' court and petty sessions used it. This Silver Street building is just one of a number of delightfully designed and thoughtfully constructed pieces of architecture that please the eye in this part of town.

Left: The proclamation of a new monarch is a strange occasion, as everyone listening in Radcliffe thought in February 1952. In one pronouncement the new queen was welcomed, but it also drew a veil over the passing of the previous incumbent on the throne. The king is dead, long live the queen seems so heartless, but it is a fact, nonetheless. Princess Elizabeth was in Kenya when the news that her father had died reached her. He had suffered ill health for some time, having been diagnosed with lung cancer the previous year. Even so, it must have come as a shock to realise that overnight you were now Elizabeth II, by the grace of God, of the United Kingdom of Great Britain and Northern Ireland and of her other realms and territories Queen, head of the Commonwealth, Defender of the Faith, to put it into a rather large nutshell. At least she had been able to prepare for her accession to the throne, having been aware since the end of 1936 that one day she would be sitting there. George VI, however, had little time to consider the role, only being thrust into the glare of the spotlight he detested at short notice when his brother abdicated both the throne and his responsibilities. King George was laid to rest on 15 February 1952. Three generations of queens mourned his passing, his mother Mary, wife Elizabeth and daughter Elizabeth II.

Below: Queen Elizabeth II came to Radcliffe in 1968 and visited Bradley Fold. She toured several sites in the area, including the internationally famous company of Dobson and Barlow. Founded in 1790, it was probably the world's first specialist textile machinery maker. Dobson and Barlow moved to Bradley fold from Bolton in 1906, continuing to flourish there until the 1980s when the operation was closed and relocated at Accrington. The visitors' book from 1968, somewhere in the company archives, contains the important entry, 'Elizabeth R'. Her time at the works caused great excitement among the employees. Even in that swinging decade, we had a love and respect for the Royal Family that time has tarnished a little. However, it has been her children and some of their unfortunate liaisons that have attracted criticism. There has never been a whiff of scandal or controversy attached to her name. She had been our queen for 16 years when she came to Radcliffe and we were proud to have such a stable monarchy in the light of all that was going on elsewhere in the world. Students rioted in the streets of Paris, Senator Bobby Kennedy was murdered in Los Angeles, South Africa refused to let Basil D'Oliveira come and play cricket because of his colour and Russian tanks rolled into Prague. God save the Queen!

At leisure

Below: Prestwich takes its name from a corruption of the old Saxon, meaning 'priest's retreat', not that these youngsters in the foreground were too worried about ancient derivations. They were too engrossed in the present. They squatted on the grass to enjoy a picnic during the 1956 Prestwich Carnival. Some flopped down on coats, others brought blankets and one or two had groundsheets to protect their white dresses from the damp. The children tucked into Shippam's potted meat paste sandwiches, washed down with lashings of Jusoda or Vimto. There were cake stands, craft stalls and games of skill to play. One such game involved trying to pass a metal hoop along a wire without touching it and sounding a buzzer. One of the Morris men providing a display can be seen in his traditional costume making his way through the crowd on the right. With bells on his trousers and stick in his hand, he would perform for people who were both interested and amused by the slightly bizarre dance done to the sound of a squeezebox. It was all part of the fun and Morris men provided a link with some pagan rituals of days gone by. A common feature of many of the dances is that of a group of men attendant on a god who celebrates his revival after death. Happily, Morris men continue to practise their art at shows today. Mummers, actors staging plays about St George or featuring doctors removing all sorts of paraphernalia from a patient's insides during a mock operation, often accompany them.

Below: The sun shone brightly on the crowd enjoying the racing and it was certainly a case of shirtsleeve weather for most of the spectators. Some of those leaning forward and clutching race order programmes probably had a personal interest in the race currently taking place. Maybe it was a family member on the way to bringing home another little trophy for the mantelpiece. The blazered officials had to keep their jackets on as a mark of their importance, but also note the number of men who still wore their ties on such a recreational occasion. Their baggy trousers with wide turn-ups tell us that this was 1953, a few years before drainpipes came into fashion with the sort of trouser leg width that meant a youth had to be shoe-horned into his choice of clothing. Ladies' skirts hung loose and well below knee length, while their hair was neatly waved and permed. Coming to watch the Agecroft Regatta was a lovely way to spend a summer's afternoon down by the river and the reader might be excused for looking at the marquee and thinking, 'Is there honey still for tea?' as Rupert Brooke once famously wrote about Grantchester. Watching oarsmen on the river is a typically British pastime, for why else would we tune in to the television to watch a pair of university eights do battle on the Thames each spring?

Woodfields was once the site of harmless fun rather than yet another retail park that the world of commerce thinks we must have. Bury Fair was a grand occasion, with its stalls, rides and thrills. During the daytime all the family had the chance to enjoy trying to shoot little metal ducks with an air rifle that had sights carefully shifted just off centre. The coconuts had a steadfast resolve, not to mention a dab of glue, that helped them stay in place even when the burliest of men hit them amidships with a wooden ball. Before the war, there were boxing booths where young men could try their luck against a seasoned old pro with cauliflower ears. The big wheel provided thrills aplenty in the days before massive roller coasters at theme parks became the norm. Candyfloss and toffee apples stickied the fingers of youngsters beaming as they carried home a goldfish in a little plastic bag, won by throwing three darts into separate playing cards. Do-gooders from misery land would do away with such prizes in 2004, leaving children and the household cat with one treat less. At night, teenagers came into their element as they tried to catch the attention of the opposite sex. Girls screamed as greasy haired lads with earrings leapt from car to car collecting their fares, giving each waltzer car an extra spin as they went. Over on the dodgems the roof sparked with electricity as lads targeted girls they fancied and bumped them amidships.

As an island nation we have a proud tradition of performing well on water, both the fresh and salt varieties. Our naval exploits are part of our heritage, thanks to the derring-do of the likes of Francis Drake and Horatio Nelson. In more recent times, the late 60s and early 70s were notable for round the world exploits. Francis Chichester, Alec Rose, Robin Knox-Johnston and Chay Blyth all achieved remarkable individual success. There was even a chance for our prime minister to make his mark on the aquatic front. In 1971, Edward Heath captained the sloop 'Morning Cloud' as part of the British team success in the Admiral's Cup. This century has given us Ellen MacArthur from landlocked Derbyshire, the fastest woman to sail round the world, recording the second quickest ever time in the prestigious Vendee Globe race. She is a member of the fairer, but not weaker, sex. In 1953, these participants in the regatta on the Irwell were trying to show their prowess on an inland watercourse, rather than at sea. Perhaps the likes of the multi medalled Olympians, Stephen Redgrave or Matthew Pinsent, began their rowing careers in such a fashion. It looks to be a close race as two little girls near the jetty clutch at one another in excitement. They were proper lasses with their frocks and white ankle socks, rather than the unisex T-Shirt and jeans of later years.

Halls of fame

Mention the Cadbury Trebor Bassett factory and lots of older locals may look a little blank. Ask them about the Adams site and they may look equally puzzled. But ask them about Hall's and that frown of concentration instantly clears to be replaced by a smile of understanding; after all hasn't everyone in the world heard of Halls' Mentholyptus cough sweets? And hundreds, indeed thousands, of Bury folk have earned their livings there down the decades churning out, amongst other products, millions upon millions of Halls' world-famous Mentholyptus cough sweets, guaranteed to give instant relief from runny noses and clogged sinuses everywhere.

Local brothers, Norman Smith Hall and Thomas Harold Hall, founded the Halls business in 1893. Norman and Thomas were appointed as joint Managing Directors of the company when the business formally became a private limited company in 1912. Thomas retired in 1926 and Norman continued as sole Managing Director until his death in 1946 when he was succeeded by his only son Roland Hall who had joined the firm in 1912, becoming a Director ten years later. Roland Hall would remain in charge until the 1960s.

The original business Hall Brothers and, later Hall Bros. (Whitefield) Ltd, began its manufacturing operations on the outskirts of Manchester, initially making soap and jam (separately we presume!) before moving into confectionery and, in 1918, moving to Stanley Road, Whitefield.

The firm's early growth was triggered by the manufacture of high quality boiled sweets. Soon the demand for

Top: *The first Directors of Hall Brothers.*
Below: *Hall Bros Bankside Works.*
Right: *Early price lists.*

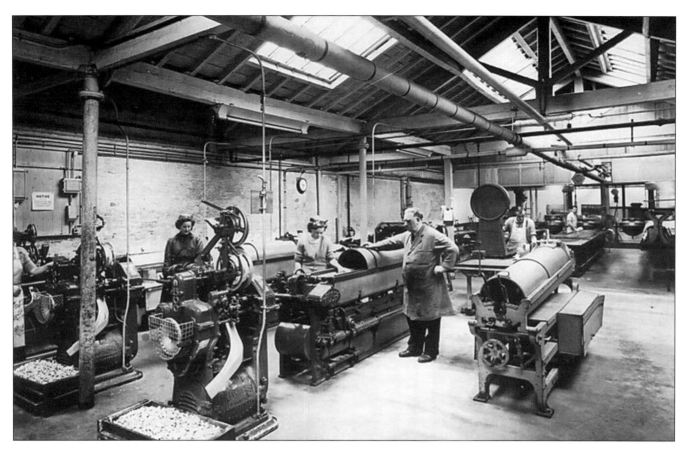

Halls confectionery had outstripped that for jam and soap. By 1924 both original products had been discarded, allowing the company to concentrate entirely on its best selling products - boiled sugar confectionery such as Halls After Dinner Mints and caramels such as Halls Dairy Gleam Caramels.

Despite the economic crash of the late 1920s, and the Depression of the next decade, the company's growth continued during the early 1930s with the introduction

Top: The boiling room circa 1930s.
Above: The company's first van.
Right: Halls Broadway Assortments and Kendal Mints.

of a new line. In 1927 the company began manufacturing Halls Mentholyptus, a high boiled sugar sweet flavoured with a unique blend of menthol and eucalyptus oil.

The product became the world's best known, best selling, cough drop and helped pave the way for the company's future growth. In 1953 the company went public, with its shares traded on the Stock Market for the first time in the year before sweet rationing came to a belated end.

In fact despite the end of sweet rationing the post war years were not particularly good ones for Halls: not least because of sugar shortages, not to mention other difficulties. Average weekly production had dropped to a mere 80 tons down from 800 tons a week before the war. Inevitably supplies of Menthol crystals from China and Brazil, and Eucalyptus oil from China and Spain, had suffered disruption after years of world conflict.

The main raw material is of course sugar. Supplies of sugar arrived in Radcliffe by tanker. In this period Government control of many prices,

including sugar, was the norm. The Sugar Board attempted to stabilise prices by the application of a Sugar Surcharge when the world price fell below the agreed Commonwealth price. During 1964 the world price was higher than the Commonwealth price for the first time in 35 years, leading to a payment to manufacturers by the Sugar Board rather than a surcharge. Before April 1964 when goods manufactured from sugar had been subject to this subsidy were exported, the subsidy received was then refunded to the Board. By the provisions of the 1964 Budget however, any such repayments which had not yet been subject to formal assessment by the Board were waived. As a result the company received a healthy £17,000 it had not expected to retain - more than a quarter of a million pounds in today's money, and a welcome opportunity to invest in increasing automation.

annual sales reaching £1.2 million - more than £20 million at today's prices. Good times were back, with the almost 400 production staff operating the factory in double shifts in the run up to Christmas 1964.

Back then workers at the factory were paid basic trade union rates plus increases for merit and skill at rates determined by time and motion studies. Canteen facilities were provided at Stanley Road. Hourly paid employees in the 1960s received two weeks paid holiday plus Bank Holidays, though those who had served for more than ten years were entitled to an extra three days holiday, and those who had put in more than 15 years a whole week's extra paid holiday.

By the mid 1960s Halls' products accounted for about a third of the entire UK market for medicated sweets,

However, whether because of, or despite such Government interference in sugar, prices gradually decreased as production began to increase and by the end of 1964 output had doubled to reached 160 tons per week,

Top: Where the boiled sugar confectionery was allowed to cool, the area know as the coolzone.
***Above:** Halls vast selection of confectionery in the 1950s.*

every other medicated sweet, with the trade name Mentho-lyptus registered in no fewer than 38 countries, though with exports concentrated mainly on the USA - and, rather more unexpectedly, Thailand.

The premises in Stanley Road covered some 4,800 square yards and included 77,000 square feet of floor space made up of the original premises used for manufacturing, plus a four storey building used for packing and warehousing and a three storey building erected in 1953 in which could be found warehousing and loading facilities on the ground floor, the tablet department on the first floor and a wrapping machine room on the second floor.

largely made up of the company's famous Mentholyptus sweets with the additional manufacture of similar products such as 'Lemo-lyptus' and 'Dr Smith's Coughs', each largely based on the same original formula, though differing in colouring and flavouring to cater for variations in the public's taste. Halls' Mentholyptus tablets outsold

The business had occupied the premises in Stanley Road, Whitefield since 1918, however, a disastrous fire on 19th February 1964 which destroyed the four storey block of the plant meant that the business had to move. Initially production was moved to a temporary location at Bankside Mill, Stand Lane, Radcliffe, though it soon moved back to Stanley Road. There a

Top left and above left: *Opening the mould of the World Largest Cough Drop, pictured above left.* ***Below:*** *The packing room.*

new four storey packing and warehousing building of brick and steel with pre-cast floor units and asphalt floor coverings was erected to replace the destroyed building at a cost of £50,000. A separate building housed the offices.

The site became impractical for the new style of continuous cooking process due to it being on four floors and soon additional space was required. The decision was taken to move to Dumers Lane in 1969.

Even the setback of the fire failed to slow the progress of Hall Brothers. Later that same year the company was acquired in a take-over bid by Warner-Lambert which recognised Hall Brothers reputation for high quality products as complimentary to its existing health-care operation.

Subsequently Warner-Lambert would operate in three core business segments: ethical pharmaceuticals, non-prescription healthcare products (known in the business as OTC, or 'over the counter' products) and confectionery. In 1971 Halls joined the Adams family, Adams being a trading name of the American Chicle Group owned by Warner-Lambert.

Hall Brothers (Whitefield) Ltd would continue as the company name until 1990 when the Radcliffe plant officially became Warner-Lambert Confectionery Ltd, though happily the change of company name did not end the Hall's brand name which lived on in the company's products. In the early 1990s the Hall's name still featured on famous products being sold in over a dozen countries, not just Britain and the USA but also

Canada, Italy, Greece, Spain and Portugal.

In 1997 Warner-Lambert would change the name of its US confectionery business from the American Chicle Group to Adams, a move designed to unify all of Warner-Lambert's international confectionery business under a single world-wide brand name.

Over the years the 'Halls' plant was responsible for many product innovations and introductions into the marketplace. Centre filled throat care products, sugar free cough drops and menthol free sweets all originated from this factory.

In addition the plant became a recognised 'centre of excellence' within the 'Halls' manufacturing community, exporting best practices worldwide and gaining a number of national accolades including MRP Class A, ISO 900 and Investors in People.

But the world of multi-national business is one which is full of corporate twists and turns.

Top right: *A birds eye view of the works.*
Above: *Damaged caused by the fire in 1964.*
Left: *Distribution of Halls sweets.*

breath fresheners - and of course Halls Cough Drops with 80 per cent of Halls production being exported to the USA through the Kaymart distribution network.

In 2003 Cadbury Schweppes main UK operating business, Cadbury Trebor Bassett, announced that it was to close the Halls Radcliffe factory when the site lease expired. Production would largely transfer to other Cadbury sites in the Americas, closer to the major 'Halls' markets, making use of spare manufacturing capacity at these facilities. Production would cease by the end of 2004 with the site closing completely in March 2005, with the sad loss of approximately 300 jobs.

In 2000 Warner-Lambert was itself acquired by Pfizer, the famous owner of the even more famous Viagra, in a $90 billion deal which created the largest pharmaceutical company in the world by far.

Two years later Pfizer, understandably more interested in drugs than confectionery, announced its intention to sell off parts of the business it had acquired from Warner-Lambert. In particular Pfizer intended to sell off Adams, and Schick-Wilkinson, Warner-Lambert's shaving products company which had been acquired in 1971.

A buyer was found for Adams in 2003. Cadbury Schweppes bought Adams for $4.2 billion to become the world's largest manufacturer of confectionery, and the world's second largest manufacturer of chewing gum.

But for local folk around Bury 'Halls' will always be remembered with affection: the factory was somewhere where generations worked, many people worked there all their lives; many found their future marriage partners there and even lived to see there own children join the firm - sometimes even their grandchildren.

But 'Halls' and those who worked for the successive companies that have owned the business have not simply made their impact on the local scene; nationally and internationally the name of Halls, and alongside it that of Radcliffe, have become familiar around the whole world. Truly everyone who ever worked there can say that they once really did work in the Halls of Fame!

Cadbury Schweppes is a major global company that manufactures, markets and distributes branded beverages and confectionery products around the world. With its own origins in the late 18th century, now after more than 200 years, Cadbury brands include Dairy Milk chocolate, Trebor Mints, Hollywood and Dandy gum as well as what had been Adams' Trident and Dentyne chewing gums, Bubbli-cious bubble gum, Certs Mints, Clorets

Top left: *An early view of the shop floor.* ***Right:*** *A birds eye view of Adams Dumers Lane, Radcliffe, factory.*

Shopping spree

From the Maypole dairy on the left and down almost its full expanse, The Rock was humming with shoppers on this day in 1950. The centrally placed streetlights, suspended on wires from standards on the pavement, add a touch of 'olde worlde' to the photograph. Lamps held within concrete posts were still a few years away. When this scene was captured we were at the exact halfway point of the century. In 1900 the 20th century dawned with a monarch coming to the end of her reign. War was raging in South Africa, trade unions formed the beginnings of the Labour party and an international exhibition was held in Paris. In 1950 our monarch was in his last years, a war began in Korea, the Labour party was in government and preparations were made for the Festival of Britain to be held the following year. There were some similarities it seems with life in late Victorian times, but the differences were far more numerous. In 1900 there were no aeroplanes, radio, television, widespread use of electricity, penicillin, X rays or atomic fission. We had come a long way, though there was still much to do, especially in putting the 'Great' back into Britain as we tried to undo the economic harm of two world wars.

Above: The little red and white striped barber's pole on the top of James Blakemore's ladies and gents hairdresser's shop is a link with the days when barbers doubled up as emergency surgeons and dentists. The very thought sends a shudder down the spine, though it could have been worse if Sweeney Todd's name appeared above the door. Established in 1906, the Bolton Street shop still offers a similar service today, though with a better lit and cleaner interior than the one seen on 17 December 1957. Richard's gents' hairdressing by Stephanie Powell currently has these premises. To the left you can now get Tasty Options, but it used to be the Evening Chronicle Offices where adverts for the Manchester paper could be lodged. Of the Manchester soccer clubs, it was known to favour City, with its rival, the Evening News, leaning more towards Old Trafford. The Evening Chronicle was first published in 1887. William Berry (1879-1954), son of a Merthyr Tydfil estate agent, established Allied Newspapers in 1924 with his brother, Gomer, acquired a number of newspapers and journals, including the Evening Chronicle. It ceased publication in 1963, the year United won the FA Cup against Leicester. Some of the names etched on the shop window are throwbacks to this era, with Sunday Graphic, Empire News and Daily Dispatch conjuring up memories of the news of around half a century ago.

Below: Rochdale Road was dotted with little shops in 1951, including Preston's sweets and tobacconist's. Inside, half of it was given over to every child's joy and source of tooth decay. Large jars of boiled sweets, dolly mixtures and fruit drops stood on shelves above the counter. The shopkeeper was quite happy to mix and match, measuring one ounce of this and another of that onto his scales. The sweets were then tipped up into a little paper bag, given a twist and passed over to the youngster whose eyes were bulging out of his head. For a few coppers more, sitting in trays, there was loose confectionery and wrapped bars that just begged to be bought and eaten. Penny Arrow bars, halfpenny fruit salad chews and sherbet fountains got everyone slavering at the thought of the lovely sensation awaiting the tongue of a prospective purchaser. There were Bassett's Allsorts to enjoy and licorice sticks to nibble, not to mention jelly babies of which the boys were better than the girls as you got a little bit extra, as the old joke went. Smokers had their own piece of heaven, with subtle aromas of loose tobacco wafting up their nostrils. Inexperienced pipe smokers dithered between St Bruno and the little whirls of Three Nuns, while the more practised reached for the thick twist that they cut with a knife and packed down using a horny, blackened thumb.

Above: The sign on the lamppost and the road designation often puzzled visitors to Bury. The A58 takes you to Heywood and eventually Rochdale, along Rochdale Road, but the quicker way to Rochdale town centre is along The Rock, to the left, and then out on Rochdale Old Road. Still, who cares about anyone wanting to leave Bury behind? In 1958 the ladies passing Dewhurst's butcher's shop wore their coats at about shin length. The skirts underneath were not much shorter and many young women favoured going to the dancehall in a dress with full skirts over a starched petticoat that twirled attractively, giving a glimpse of lace as they jived to Danny and the Juniors singing 'At the hop'. Dancing was one of the attractions that loosened the purse strings for a night out and proper dancing it was, too. You could quickstep as well as jive to many of the rock and roll favourites of the day, finishing off with a bit of canoodling to a Michael Holliday or Dickie Valentine tune as the last waltz was played. The opposite sex actually touched and held one another on the dance floor, because it was only when Chubby Checker's twisting songs came along at the end of 1960 that separation came to pass. Then it was handbags in the middle and gyrate around them as in a Sioux ceremony.

Right: It is hard to imagine quite what had taken this young mum's fancy in the shop window of Mason's Motor Mart on Rochdale Road in September 1950. Surely she was not contemplating a new set of slicks for the Formula One pram she was pushing? The coat she wore reflected the style of the middle of the last century. During the war, cloth was needed for uniforms, blankets and blackout curtains and was in short supply for use in ladies' fashion. Hemlines, by necessity, rose, but when peace came the fairer sex could indulge their outfitting whims, though clothing coupons meant that they did not have complete carte blanche to indulge themselves. The tot in the pram was one of the first recipients of the welfare state ushered in by the Attlee government that won the 1945 general election. The National Health Service (NHS) was born in the summer of 1948, offering free medical treatment for the entire population and free prescriptions. Dental care, including the supply of dentures, also came within NHS provision as did free spectacles and, bizarrely, wigs. The scheme was not popular with the British Medical Association who saw the NHS as the slayer of the golden goose, not a very altruistic attitude. It had set up a fund to fight the proposals when the government first mooted them. Many doctors initially threatened to boycott the service, but the dust eventually settled and we ended up with one of the real successes of the Attlee era.

SPARES
SALES
LUCAS
PHONE
433

ACCESSORIES
MOTOR TYRES
SERVICE DEALER
BATTERIES OILS
REBORING Etc.

MACSONS MOTOR MART

Right: The memorial to John Kay, to the right, was erected on a sandstone base rescued from the old market building that stood here from 1839 until it was demolished in 1901 when the new market was opened. The chimney rising up above Bury Shopping Centre parade belongs to the School of Arts and Crafts. Serving the boiler house, the 100 foot high chimney was designed by local architect Maxwell Tuke in the style of an Italian campanile. He achieved national fame in 1895 with his 520 foot Blackpool Tower. The school opened the previous year and the Borough Engineer, Joshua Cartwright, designed its main body. Being a technical school, it marked a major leap forward in Bury's educational provision. Neighbouring land from Lord Derby's estate was acquired and landscaped by Henry Whitehead, the benefactor responsible for Kay Gardens, and laid out as Sparrow Park. The school has a number of intricate, ornamental features typical of late Victorian architecture. The friezes that JR Whittick sculpted are particularly notable as they depict the various subjects taught in the school. The photograph was taken in July 1963 and shows a nice contrast between old and new with the setts in the roadway supporting the wheels of transport that threatened to strangle our towns four decades ago and still does today.

Bottom left: Scurrying across The Rock in July 1963, the shoppers on the zebra crossing were near Fred Dawes' television rental shop. This one of a chain developed during the 1950s by a man with an eye for an opening. The first widespread call for that little flickering black and white image to be available on goggle boxes in our living rooms was largely inspired by Queen Elizabeth's Coronation. The ceremony was transmitted live and the one family in the street owning a TV set suddenly found out that it had a large number of friends who happened to call round on 2 June 1953. Almost overnight, the nation was hooked. Even though there was only one channel to watch and programmes were largely limited to evenings, this new form of home entertainment soon dominated family life. But, sets were expensive and Dawes was one of the first to recognise that renting a television was the way to make it accessible to those on a limited budget. It still makes good sense today, with the rapid advances in technology making older models obsolete in next to no time. In 1969 he sold the business to Radio Rentals, subsequently being renamed Rumbelows. At the time of this photograph, people relaxed in the evening watching 'No Hiding Place' and 'Steptoe and Son' and got their

local news from 'Scene at 6.30'. To the right, Timothy White's chemist existed until 1968 before being taken over by Boot's.

Below: This part of The Rock, with Cross Street to the left, is now a safe haven for shoppers to stroll comfortably along, without the worry of traffic surrounding them. It was a different story in 1963 as the cars streamed past Dorothy Perkins' ladies fashion and the Saxone shoe shop. Both these establishments would have to adjust their range of stock over the next few years. Women, especially those of the younger generation, were soon to indulge in something of a revolution. In January 1964 a young designer called Mary Quant opened a shop she described as a 'boutique' in Chelsea. Her bold designs and short skirts were specifically aimed at those who were tired of wearing essentially the same as their mothers. Instead of flowing, flowery dresses, teens and twenties went in for ever shorter miniskirts. Vicars were outraged and red-blooded males delighted. Saxone cleared away most of its stiletto heeled shoes that beehive headed girls used to totter about on. These lasses cut their hair shorter or let it fall about their shoulders and bought knee length boots to complement their new hemlines. There used to be four different names for the stretch of road that came to be known as The Rock. In 1923 the local Chamber of Trade requested that a common name be designated because of the confusion caused by having various names given to short sections of the street, but the official renaming did not occur until 1935.

Left: This is one of the last views of Bury Market ever taken. Little did the shoppers realise that they were sharing an experience that was to be no more after November 1968 when a disastrous fire gutted the building. Lord Derby's Market was in existence from 1839 to 1901 on land that was to become Kay Gardens. The new one opened on 13 December 1901 with 17 shops and 100 stalls all vying for custom. As well as Halstead's grocer's, Derby's butcher's and the ironmonger's belonging to James Lawless, there were several businesses decidedly local in their produce. Gosling's sold treacle toffee from trays, John Cox had his tripe and, of course, there were some devoted to the delights of the black pudding. It is confusing to talk of this as the 'new market' because, after the fire and the appearance of its replacement concrete and glass modern market off Angouleme Way, it became the 'old market'! Shopping at the market had been part of Bury life ever since the 15th century when Henry VI granted a royal charter. The first ones could only be held on specific days, partly for security reasons as merchants could travel to and from market towns in the safety of numbers as footpads lay in wait for easy pickings, hoping that a lonely trader with bulging pockets would come their way.

Below: In July 1963 the press was buzzing with the scandal of the Profumo affair as news that the Minister for War and other high ranking people were involved with call girls and posed a risk to national security. That summer, the Beatles went to the top of the charts with 'She loves you' and the public looked at Christine Keeler and Mandy Rice-Davies and said, 'Yeah, yeah, yeah'. The carriageway around Kay Gardens was heavy with traffic and pedestrians were glad of the crossing that gave them the chance to get over the road in some safety. Even over 40 years ago, congestion was a major problem as we were already well into the era when most families were car owners. Despite the raft of measures that local and national governments have imposed with pedestrianisation, one way systems, no parking areas, park and ride schemes, congestion levies etc, there still seems to be no solution to gridlock in sight. Kay Gardens, at the top of the picture, were laid out from 1903 in honour of the man who made a major contribution to the production of woven cloth. They were officially opened in 1908 by Mrs Whitehead, the wife of the donor who also provided the domed memorial erected by W Venn Gough, a Bristol sculptor of some repute. Lord Derby unveiled the 35 foot Portland stone structure later that same day.

On the home front

In 1939 Britain's Prime Minister Neville Chamberlain had made his announcement to the waiting people of Britain that '...this country is at war with Germany.' The country rolled up its sleeves and prepared for the inevitable. This war would be different from other wars. This time planes had the ability to fly further and carry a heavier load, and air raids were fully expected. Air raid shelters were obviously going to be needed, and shelters were built on open places across towns and cities. By the time war was declared an army of volunteers of both sexes had already been recruited to form an Air Raid Protection service. At first ARP personnel were unpaid volunteers but when war broke out in Septem-

ber 1939 they became paid staff. It was their job to patrol specified areas, making sure that no chinks of light broke the blackout restrictions, checking the safety of local residents, being alert for gas attacks, air raids and unexploded bombs. The exceptional work done by Air Raid Wardens in dealing with incendiaries, giving first aid to the injured, helping to rescue victims from their bombed-out properties, clearing away rubble, and a thousand and one other tasks became legendary; during the second world war nearly as many private citizens were killed as troops - and many of them were the gallant ARP wardens. At the beginning of the war Sir Anthony Eden, Secretary of State for War, appealed in a radio broadcast for men between 17 and 65 to make up a new force, the Local Defence Volunteers, to guard vulnerable points from possible Nazi attack. Within a very short time the first men were putting their names down. At first the new force had to improvise; there were no weapons to spare and men had to rely on sticks, shotguns handed in by local people, and on sheer determination . Weapons and uniforms did not become available for several months. In July the Local Defence Volunteers was renamed the Home Guard, and by the following year were a force

to be reckoned with. Television programmes such as 'Dad's Army' have unfortunately associated the Home Guard with comedy, but in fact they performed much important work. The Guard posted sentries to watch for possible aircraft or parachute landings at likely spots such as disused aerodromes, golf courses on the outskirts of towns, local parks and racecourses. They manned anti-aircraft rocket guns, liaised with other units and with regular troops, set up communications and organised balloon barrages. Other preparations were hastily made. Place names and other identifying marks were obliterated to confuse the enemy about exactly where they were. Notices went up everywhere giving good advice to citizens on a number of issues. 'Keep Mum - she's not so dumb' warned people to take care what kind of information they passed on, as the person they were speaking to could be an enemy.

Older readers will remember how difficult it was to find certain items in the shops during the war; combs, soap, cosmetics, hairgrips, elastic, buttons, zips - all were virtually impossible to buy as factories that once produced these items had been turned over to war work. Stockings were in short supply, and resourceful women resorted to colouring their legs with gravy browning or with a mixture of sand and water. Beetroot juice was found to be a good substitute for lipstick.

Clothes rationing was introduced in 1941, and everyone had 66 coupons per year. Eleven coupons would buy a dress, and sixteen were needed for a coat. The number of coupons was later reduced to 40 per person. People were required to save material where they could - ladies' hemlines went up considerably, and skirts were not allowed to have lots of pleats. Some found clever ways around the regulations by using materials that were not rationed. Blackout material could be embroidered and made into blouses or skirts, and dyed sugar sacks were turned into curtains.

Bangers sizzling and spitting in the pan, now what a delight. All throughout the summer we are used to seeing dad wheel out the gas barbecue into the garden, put on the apron he would not be seen dead in anywhere else and start issuing instructions to the kids to bring the marinated steaks to him for searing on the outside while the inside remains red raw. He would have loved it in June 1956, even if he had to make do with a pile of bricks instead of the expensive machine he bought at B & Q. But there was a serious side to this scene. These women were cooking sausages for 300 as part of a civil defence training exercise. Improvised emergency cookers

were built from bricks, tin and assorted rubble found on waste ground and supplemented by transportable kitchen equipment that included Bluff cookers, Triplex field cookers and Soyer boilers. Many of these had been put to good use during World War II, especially in bomb hit areas when casualties, the homeless and firefighters needed the support of food stations that could be quickly assembled. Cynics laughed at the Girl Guide nature of these field kitchens, but they had the smirks removed from their faces when they saw them in operation for real. This exercise was mounted to give the civil defence chance to practise its reactions in case of a missile attack by Russia.

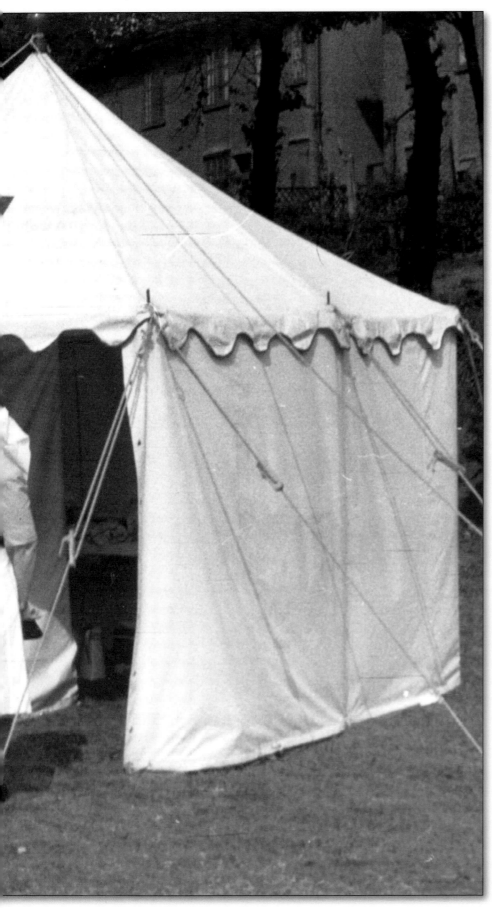

Having a quiet fag outside the first aid tent at Prestwich Carnival in 1956, this chap was eavesdropping on the nurses' conversation. Still, with five women to contend with he would not have had a chance of getting a word in edgeways, so he might just as well have resigned himself to the role of being an audience. Anyway, they would have thought that, as a man, he did not have anything intelligent to contribute, so there! What, can we imagine, had interested this group so much that it had to hold a discussion? All women like a good wedding, so maybe that was the subject involved. In April, there was a fairytale story about a beautiful girl dreaming of the day when her prince would come. She was called Grace Kelly, the American actress who was marvellous as Gary Cooper's Quaker wife in the movie 'High Noon'. Her beau was Prince Rainier, the monarch of Monaco, and they tied the knot in front of 1,200 guests. In June, there was another touch of glamour when the hourglass wed the egghead. Marilyn Monroe, with curves that a girl would kill for, went to the altar with playwright Arthur Miller. Either of those two events would have kept the nurses gossiping for ages, but they look to be much too professional to have ignored their duties.

Bird's eye view

Radcliffe is a corruption of 'red cliff', a rocky protrusion on the River Irwell. It also gave its name to the de Radeclive family who, in time, adopted the spelling as we know it today. The manor left the Radcliffes' control in the 16th century and came into the possession of Lord Grey de Wilton in the early 19th century. The 1964 aerial photograph shows the viaduct over the Irwell, to the top left, and includes a number of mill chimneys that remind us of the degree to which the area was dependent upon the paper and textile trades in former times. The town had a population of about 4,500 when Queen Victoria came to the throne, but had grown sufficiently to become an Urban District Council in 1894. At the same time, the boundary was extended to include Stand Lane and its environs. By the turn into the 20th century, the electorate totalled over 15,000, a number swollen further when Outwood and Ainsworth were brought under the council's control in 1933. A royal charter, granted by King George V in 1935, meant that Radcliffe became a municipal borough. Since the reorganisation of local government in 1974, the town's population, now standing at over 33,000, has come under the wing of Bury Metropolitan Borough.

This aerial view dates from 1933 and shows that we once had a town that did not possess a shopping mall, multi storey car parks and fast food outlets to provide us with a satisfactory way of life. To be fair, it was a completely different era. The 1930s were depressing times for many, with unemployment pushing 3 million at one stage. The volume of traffic was nothing compared that of the 21st century. Looking down from his aeroplane, the pilot had only a handful of cars in his viewfinder. Most people used public transport to get around, as instanced by the trams we can spot. Alternatively, they walked and the roads are dotted with pedestrians using that most ancient method of getting about, namely Shanks's pony. The parish church of St Mary is top left on the Wylde, by Market Place. Silver Street, with its shop awnings, runs down the photograph. On the right hand side, at the corner with Broad Street, is a lovely example of architecture created a century ago. No 19 Silver Street opened in 1904 as the Conservative Club and has delightfully carved stone statues at roof level. Just further down, on the opposite side of the street at No 26, stands Barclays Bank, with the Bank Chambers round the corner on Bank Street. Market Street runs across the picture to Kay Gardens to meet Haymarket Street.

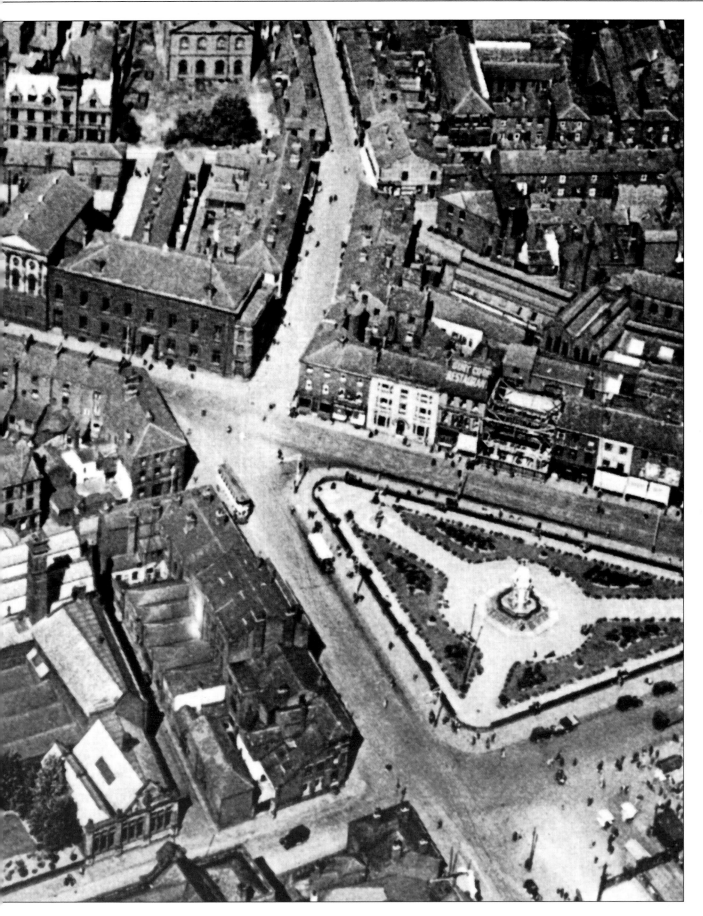

Lights, camera, action. But, this is not a film studio or a set at Pinewood. Something special, though, was being recorded for posterity, a documentary or newsreel item. A piece of willow was the star of this particular show in c1950. Together with his brother, Arnold Neely ran a family business that attracted famous sporting names to the workshop in Radcliffe. Only the finest wood was selected for the manufacture of cricket bats intended to send even the most cunning googly a spinner could send down whizzing across the grass to the boundary rope. The family also ran a sports outfitters in Church Street and a second generation, led by Alex Neely, continued the business at the aptly named Willow Works off Quarry Street until his death in 1960. These bats were lovingly made and carefully turned and planed until their balance was perfect. They were quite lightweight in comparison with the jumbo models that many cricketers use today. Individual players would visit the workshop and have bats tailormade for them, with a little extra thickness on the handle for those with large hands and a hope for little more in the sweet spot by batsmen whose timing had gone off. The sound of leather on willow never sounded as pure as when coming off a product from this local company.

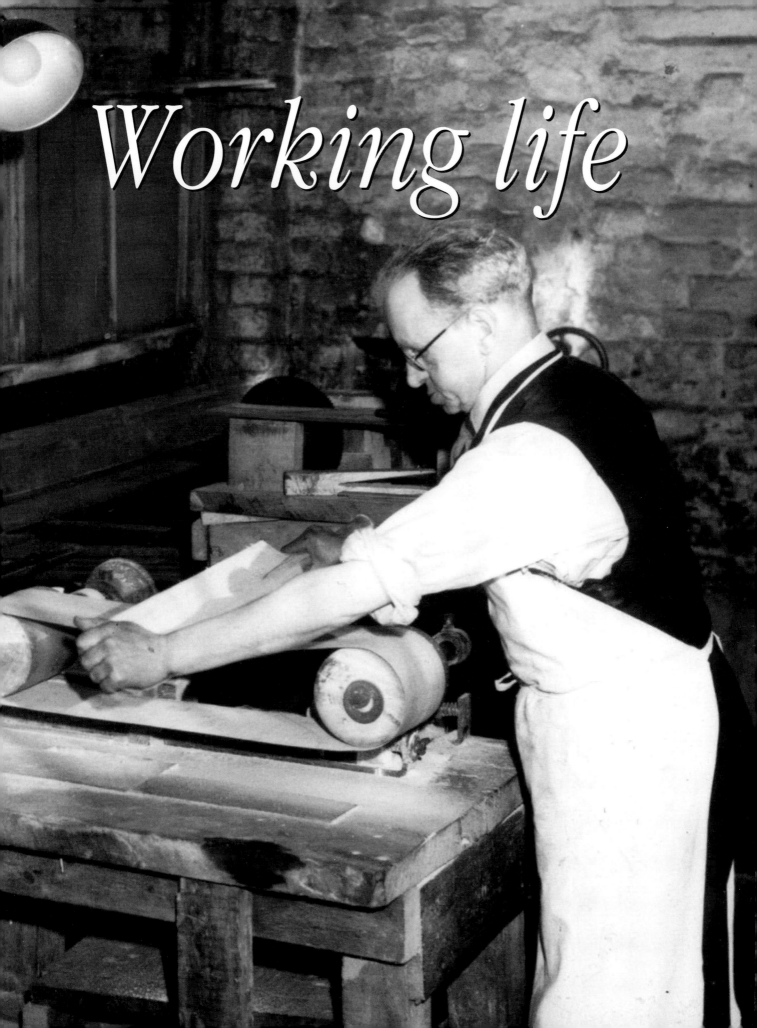

Working life

Below: Tons of earth were removed from Union Square in May 1939 as the underground air raid shelters took shape. Made of reinforced concrete, they measured 6 feet 7 inches in height and had a width of 4 feet, each accommodating 700 people. At home we were encouraged to have our own personal ones. The most common design became known as the Anderson shelter, named after the government minister. When the sirens went, people grabbed blankets and flasks of soup and settled down for an uncomfortable night with just a few candles carefully shielded so that no air raid warden had to shout 'Put that light out' as they did after blackout was introduced in the first month of the war. Still, it was better than being trapped in a bombed out house. Later in the war, the minister for home security, Herbert Morrison, was to have an indoor shelter named after him. It was more of a reinforced table than anything and did not inspire a great deal of confidence. Anyone clinging to a hope that war could be averted must have had that last straw torn from his grasp when he saw these civil defence measures being undertaken. That same month, Italy and Germany signed the political and military alliance known as the 'Pact of Steel', while at home farmers were urged to plough up grazing land and convert to food crops and arable production.

Right: We knew it was coming, even if realisation dawned rather late. The storm clouds over Europe were with us during the late 1930s and it was only a matter of time before the balloon went up, as the saying went. For a brief period, both we and our government hoped against hope and tried to take some crumb of comfort from Mr Chamberlain's little slip of paper, brought back from Munich, on which he declared that he had an agreement with Herr Hitler that guaranteed 'peace for our time'. Part of the deal was that Germany could move on Czechoslovakia and many pundits viewed the government's action as a sell out and sheer cowardice. Even members of Chamberlain's own party openly criticised him, with future prime ministers Winston Churchill, Anthony Eden and Harold Macmillan being especially vociferous. Edward Heath, then a young student, stood against Quinton Hogg in the Oxford by-election, using the slogan, 'a vote for Hogg is a vote for Hitler'. By May 1939 it was obvious even to Chamberlain that Germany had major ambitions all across Europe, including our own little island. The country tried to make up for lost time and mount some form of civil defence measures. Union Square was dug up and underground air raid shelters installed. The body language of the men watching the excavation work suggests that they were resigned to the coming of hostilities and the necessity of the shelters.

Above: In May 1941 the war was in full swing as the next issue of ration books was prepared in Radcliffe. Things were not going well and the nation felt as if it stood alone against the might of the German forces. America resisted all overtures to enter the war and Yugoslavia was overrun and Athens fell in April. The blitz on London reached its peak on 11 May when 550 enemy planes dropped high explosives and incendiaries that killed 1,400 in a single raid. There was a small crumb of comfort when we learned that the Bismarck, Germany's newest and fastest battleship, was lying at the bottom of the Atlantic after a pounding from the Ark Royal's aircraft and the guns and torpedoes from Rodney, King George V and Victorious. The ration books were got ready at a time when various schemes were tried to encourage people to salvage things, dig for victory and sponsor a Spitfire. This week it was the turn of War Weapons to be the favoured crusade. It was different from other charities in that there was no named cause. People paid money into War Bonds, Savings Certificates and Defence Bonds. Parades were held and displays mounted during War Weapons Week to publicise the drive. People were urged to save so that they could feel to be contributing to the war effort and to prevent an economic crisis from a run on the banks if there was a threat of invasion.

Below: Is Jacqueline Sandford still out there? She must be pedalling her way down to the post office today to draw her pension. Jacqueline, a resident of North Street, Radcliffe, had come from her home not far from the station to take part in a cycling proficiency rally. It was the sort of road safety measure that was desperately needed in 1950. Cars kept off the roads by petrol rationing and wartime mileage restrictions were returning to claim back the highways. Children had become used to cycling round the streets and lanes in comparative safety as they seldom had to negotiate a passing car or worry too much at a crossroads. Accident statistics, particularly among the young, were frightening. Never a day went by without a newspaper report of yet another kiddie being knocked over or run down. The 'Stop, look and listen' campaign taught children the dangers involved in crossing the road and urged them to find a safe place to use, away from parked cars. The scheme for National Cycling Proficiency was introduced and willing volunteers commandeered school playgrounds, giving instruction to the young on many aspects of using their bikes sensibly and safely. When the course was completed and a practical and oral test passed, successful candidates got a certificate to take home and a triangular metal badge to wear. Has Jacqueline still got hers, for we are sure she won one?

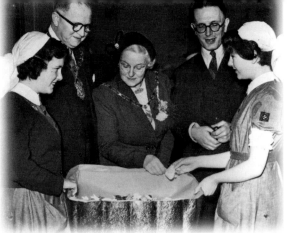

Right: In Britain we have long had a tradition of spending hour upon hour in trying to raise small amounts of money to help fund organisations such as schools, charities and societies. Although such efforts produce a mere drop in the ocean, we continue to run bring and buy stalls, jumble sales and mock auctions. This approach had its benefits in the war years when we collected scrap iron, rags and paper for the effort against the enemy, but the 'mend and make do' mentality still persists in peacetime and an age of prosperity. Back in 1955, Radcliffe's St John Ambulance Brigade held its Autumn Fair. We hope that the man on the right did not knock his pipe out in the lucky dip tub or he might have found himself in need of some urgent medical attention from the young attendants. St John Ambulance, and not 'St John's' as people often say incorrectly, is a regular contributor to sporting venues, carnivals and anywhere there is a large gathering likely to need some medical attention. St John Ambulance began in the great days of the British Empire, quickly spreading to our overseas colonies. Queen Victoria made the British Order of St John a Royal Order of Chivalry and in 1887 trained volunteers were formed into a uniformed brigade to provide first aid and an ambulance service at public events. Its first official wartime role was in the Boer War and an extensive service of hospitals and medical services in World War I was run by the Joint War Committee of the Red Cross and St John Ambulance.

Below: In the mid 1950s we were in the middle of the Cold War, that time when there was a real fear that things would turn very hot indeed. The threat of nuclear attack and the devastation that would cause was taken very seriously. People spoke of four minute warnings and practised their responses to a potential disaster. This picture was taken in June 1956 at Radcliffe's civil defence headquarters. Although the organisation's name suggests response by civilians to enemy attack, there were other occasions when survival and rescue skills were needed. In August 1952 a disastrous flood devastated the Devon resort of Lynmouth, killing 36 and making thousands homeless. All that training came to good effect as the Red Cross, Women's Voluntary Service and other groups leapt into immediate action, providing much needed support for families and the emergency services. The activity was repeated the following February when the east coast was hit by hurricane winds, torrential rain and the collapse of sea defences. The civil defence team at Radcliffe and all other centres took their responsibilities seriously and practised evacuation procedures and the setting up of relief camps. Everyone hoped that there would be no need for the call to action for real but, just in case, each was ready and willing to do whatever was asked.

Handing on the light

The educational establishment, now known as Holy Cross, has been through many metamorphoses since its inception in 1878.

Let us take you back to Germany and the 'Kulturkampf' in the 19th Century. At the same time as Otto von Bismarck was trying to get rid of teachers who were religiously inclined Cardinal Vaughan of the Salford Diocese was searching for them. The Congregation of the Daughters of the Cross was founded in Liege, Belgium in 1833 and by 1851 had extended to Germany. Sisters, happily teaching in Germany now found themselves banished. By happy coincidence Cardinal Vaughan's search was underway and in 1878 some of those same sisters found themselves in Bury. None of this was easy for them though: on arrival they were without even the bare necessities such as chairs and tables and cups and saucers. However, by dint of starting a school in a very small way and charging pupils a penny a week, as well as recruiting assistance from the people of Bury, they were able to gather together the essentials. The cramped conditions in a little house in Bank Street necessitated a move to Derby House, further down Manchester Road, and very soon another move further down again to The Ferns, a building which remains part of the present College.

Education for all was a relatively new idea in those days, and as the Sisters expanded their property from The Ferns new demands were made on them, for example that of training of pupil teachers. As these trainees came from other parts of the country and from Ireland, they needed a place to live: thus the boarding school was born. Along the way a very beautiful Chapel, described as 'puginesque' and a gem of its kind was built - now sadly demolished to make room for the Maureen Haverty building.

Sister Iphigenie from Germany, who was the driving force behind all that happened in the early days at Bury had a dream that she might have a little college on site

Above: Children at Ashworth Valley in 1883.
Below: Children pose for a photograph in 1900.

for the training of good teachers. This was separate from the pupil teacher programme. In 1999 Sister Iphigenie's dream would at last become a reality when, in conjunction with Liverpool Hope University, adult provision at the College at last arrived, helping prepare many people for a career in the world of education.

Another idea that would come full circle is the name. The foundation stone of the Holy Cross School was laid back in 1887 in the Golden Jubilee of Queen Victoria's reign. Other names would be used in subsequent decades, but in 1979 when the college was being founded the title Holy Cross College was the one that found universal favour.

In 1905 the school ceased to be a public elementary school and began work as a secondary school: the preparatory school for the younger pupils functioned separately. The secondary school was entitled to grants from the Board of Education. Money was obtained from various other sources and buildings erected about that time are still very serviceable today. In 1910 however, a great fire damaged the boarding school at the top and back of Summerfield, adjacent to The Ferns. Records tell us that the rebuilding and refurbishment costs were £500. Grants became available over the years enabling further improvement. The sixth form started in 1920, followed by the purchase of Agincourt in 1922 and the playing fields next door soon after. Agincourt has now been demolished to make way for the latest building planned to open at Christmas 2004 whilst part of the playing fields has had to make way for yet another new building.

Lest this became a litany of buildings and money, let us pause for a moment to think of the enormous human

benefit that has resulted from all these efforts. Holy Cross has been fortunate in the wonderful head-teachers who have graced the school over the years. They have enriched the

Top left: *A Classroom in 1907.*
Above: *An early 20th century dormitory.*
Below: *The school Art Room, 1935.*

lives of scores of pupils, students and staff and made Bury a better place by their presence and effort. The religious significance of their lives of service has added to the growth in spirituality of hundreds of people. In all its successes it has held on firmly to these truths and the beauty of its motto 'All knowledge comes from God'.

Readers who attended the school in the 1930s may recall 'the year of three kings'. The year 1936 began with pupils mourning the death of a King then celebrating the proclamation of another; trying to make sense of his abdication, and eventually celebrating the Coronation of King George VI and Queen Elizabeth.

And if the abdication crisis was not enough to puzzle young minds what of war with all its scares, tribulations and deprivations? Those in charge of the school simply looked ahead and worked out an elaborate and imaginative building

programme that would be put in place when peace returned. In 1944 Holy Cross became a Direct Grant School, known as Bury Convent Grammar School. When the war ended in 1945 numbers began to increase.

The Boarding School closed in 1950 to make room for the rapidly expanding day school. The long-awaited building programme swung into action and has not ceased since. The sixth form that started with single figures in the early 1920s grew to between two and three hundred. The school roll shot up to over seven hundred.

Top: *The Emilie Mary Building pictured in 1952.*
Above: *Girls enjoying a game of netball in the school playing fields.* **Left:** *School leavers of 1973.*

efforts, sending the College well on its way to enjoying well-deserved state of the art facilities.

There was a time when 700 girls aged 11-18 seemed to be the maximum for the campus: today there are 1400 students aged 16-19. But that is not all: there are many people in our area who, for one reason or another, left formal education early but who would now like to return to it; Holy Cross has the facilities to help them do so. In conjunction with Liverpool Hope University, Holy Cross decided to use slack periods such as evenings to provide degree, diploma or other forms of extended education. That initiative flourished and now more than five hundred local people take advantage of the courses.

The College now rejoices in the fact that it has been placed amongst the top sixth form colleges in the country and has been awarded Beacon Status.

None of the developments which have taken place down the years however could have happened without the courage and bravery of those first Sisters who arrived in Bury in 1878. In the fullness of time their place was taken by devoted Heads and staff who appreciated the mission of the Founders and built on the spiritual ethos they passed down. That mission and ethos is still palpable today. Whatever the future may hold today's staff are well aware that they are the custodians of a precious inheritance and their task is to keep that torch alight, and in their turn too to pass it on.

Yet major changes were soon on the horizon. In the late 1970s the Government decided that direct grant schools were no longer an option. Three choices were available: the school could close, it could go 'independent' or, thirdly, join forces with the Local Authority. The school authorities chose the latter option and so far have not regretted it. The outcome of all the discussions on reorganisation was that the school would become an open-access co-educational Sixth Form College. It was felt however that the young men who came to the college would not want to admit that they attended a Convent establishment so a new name was needed. It took little deliberation to decide to revert to the original name of Holy Cross College.

Meanwhile the Government decided that a body called the Further Education Funding Council should take over responsibility for post-16 colleges. Effectively, the College was now out of the control of the Local Education Authority. Holy Cross' new bosses had such a weird and wonderful way of working out funding that it defied the intelligence of all but the smartest. The simple fact was that the College did not have enough money and it had a few hard years. Since funding was historically based, the well-off authorities did well, but Bury had to wait for 'convergence' which came in over a few years. And happily another set of bosses 'the Learning and Skills Council' came in to look after the College. Money has however, come from several different sources, much through the College's own fund raising

Top left: Mature students take advantage of the evening courses provided by Holy Cross.
Above left: Bury Convent Grammar School.
Below: Holy Cross reception area, 2004.

A billion dollar package

There can't be many businesses operating in Bury that can claim to be part of a multi national business with a billion dollars a year turnover. Nor can there be many businesses in the town which can claim an uninterrupted history of going back almost three centuries. Yet today's Printpack, the packaging firm based in Bridge Hall Mills, can place a tick in both boxes.

Perhaps surprisingly, packaging has been the foundation of a number of great fortunes in the second half of the 20th century. For younger readers buying food in printed packages is the normal way that food is supplied: older readers however, will recall that things were not always so.

Until the 1950s and 60s it was still commonplace to have food of all kinds displayed loose and to ask the shop keeper for say a pound of sugar, and for it to be weighed out and then poured into a paper bag. These days of course food of almost all kinds is pre-packed in pre-printed cartons or in printed plastic bags or wrappers.

It was the advent of the supermarket, taking over from the traditional sole trader, which spurred the change in packaging.

Top: *James Erskine Love Jr, founder of Printpack.*
Right: *Bridge Hall Mills in the 18th century.*
Below: *An aerial view of Bridge Hall Mills, 1924.*

30th April 1928 for £65,000, and new machinery was soon installed to manufacture acetate film or 'cellophane' the latter name incidentally being a trademark which had been registered by its inventor, Swiss chemist, JE Brandenburger, in 1908.

Acetate film was manufactured from a compound of cellulose and acetic acid and technically known as acetyl-cellulose or cellulose acetate. A new acetate plant was erected during 1929 and production finally got underway that Autumn. Acetate was however relatively expensive to produce and production would very soon shift to the cheaper viscose film. By 1930 the fledgling new business was beginning to find its feet, a position which all too soon would be undermined by the years of economic recession.

Brown paper bags were out and in came cellophane and plastic. And yet this story of one the world's most successful purveyors of plastic packaging begins with paper.

They had begun making paper at Bury's Bridge Hall Mills in the early 1700s. In the 19th century Bridge Hall Mills was one of the largest paper mills in Britain, but paper making was first recorded there as early as 1716 when the tenant of the mill was one George Warburton.

During the 19th century a large mill complex grew under the ownership of George Wrigley & Son, a factory which at its height in the 1880s employed almost 500 local folk.

Alas the good times could not last and the paper mill closed in 1924 - apparently forever.

The origins of the present day flexible packaging manufacturing by Printpack can be traced to the Transparent Paper Company in the 1920s. 'TP' Ltd, or 'Tranny' as the firm was known locally, started the process of manufacturing cellulose film (clear paper) at Bridge Hall Mills in Bury in 1928.

The freehold of the Mills was bought by Transparent Paper on

Though the outbreak of war in 1939 would inevitably see a further fall in production as raw materials became scarce, the Bridge Hall Mills remained fully occupied as contracts for war work came in. Some 200,000 square feet of factory space would be given over to war production. Contracts were received at the mills for the manufacturing of cartridge containers: by February 1942 work began on building the gluing, winding and cutting machines to produce those tubular cardboard cartons. By the end of the war over six million containers had been produced.

The cardboard tube business would continue after the war, with the Tubular Case and Carton Company being created as a subsidiary of Transparent Paper Ltd.

Top: A derelict Bridge Hall Mill in 1928. **Right:** *Transparent Paper Ltd, circa 1930.*

Expansion would come in the post war world. Part of the Mills had been destroyed by fire late in 1944. Though little had changed at the Mills since 1915 a new finishing section was completed in 1947. A programme of new building and investment in equipment would continue over the next ten years. Investment between 1954 and 1956 would double the plant's capacity

To improve its sales of 'cello' TP Ltd now started to 'convert' or print on the film with the construction of the conversion plant in the 1950s - this would be the basis of the current business which in the post war years would grow dramatically from having some 450 employees in 1956 to a peak of some 1,600 in 1960.

In those days the manufacture of cellulose film was a rather smelly process due to the chemicals used: something many readers may recall. Happily, by contrast, manufacturing today is odour free, with no impact on the local environment.

In the 1970s cellophane started to be replaced by plastic; the world-wide decline in demand for cellophane resulted in the closure of the cello plant on 1982.

Polythene had made its first appearance at Bridge Hall Mills in the early 1950s at which time Transparent Paper had

created a subsidiary, Flexible Packaging Ltd, to develop and sell this new product, though it soon sold it off as unprofitable.

Two decades later however the focus of Transparent Paper would shift back to the printing and conversion of flexible plastic packaging.

Following the closure of the cello plant in 1982 the business passed through the hands of a number of different owners in the 1980s and early 1990s. In 1993 it was finally acquired by Printpack Inc. of Atlanta, Georgia, in the USA. The business has since thrived as part of the Printpack family.

Printpack was founded in Atlanta by James Erskine Love Jr in 1956. It remains privately owned by the Love family headed by Erskine's eldest son Dennis as Company President; Erskine's widow, Gay, remains Chairman.

To get his small firm afloat back in the mid 1950s Erskine had used every available asset he possessed: equity in his home, his car and even

Top right: *Production of jettison fuel tanks during the years of the Second World War.* ***Above right and left:*** *Pre and post war views inside the Slitting Department.*

the surrender value of his life insurance. He did not possess a single dollar which was not put into the business. Then with an equal amount of money - $60,000 - borrowed from the bank he started the business with his wife and his father.

Producing cellophane wrappers, and soon afterwards printing those same wrappers, would prove to have been an astonishingly shrewd move.

To begin with Erskine Love was his company's sole employee, though soon John Sample, blind in one eye and as a result rejected by the Bell Telephone company, joined Erskine. By March 1957 Erskine was advising the bank that he expected to be able to pay off the loan within a matter of weeks, and shortly thereafter the number of employees grew to ten. In that first full year sales amounted to $26,000, by 1959 the company was reporting an annual turnover of $1,300,000, a year later that had grown by a further half million dollars; that expansion would continue both by growth and purchases for thirty and more years, and in due course lead the Love family to Britain in search of new acquisitions

Erskine Love died of a massive heart attack in 1987 at the age of just 59; he had lived to see his once small company grow to be an industry giant. All five of Erskine Love's sons however, would be involved in the business. In the UK Erskine's fourth son, Bill, was Sales and Marketing Director for five years prior to his tragic death at the age of just 41

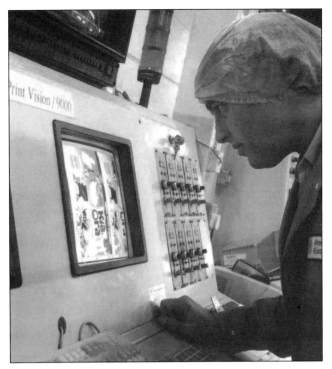

when his plane crashed into Mount Kenya in Africa in 2003. Bill Love's wife, daughter and nine other members of his wife's family also died in the crash.

Today Printpack is firmly focused on flexible packing, turning over more than a billion dollars annually, and with 23 manufacturing plants in North America, Mexico and Europe.

The headquarters of the European business is Bridge Hall Mills, Bury, with another plant in Saffron Walden in Essex.

The UK operation has a £60 million annual turnover with 330 employees, of whom some 230 are based in Bury. Today the business supplies high quality printed flexible packaging for wrapping crisps, snacks, biscuits, confectionery and for labelling carbonated soft drinks bottles. Printpack's main customers are major food and beverage manufacturers such

as Walkers Crisps, KP Foods, McVities, Burtons Biscuits, Coca Cola, Fox's Biscuits, Cadbury and Nestle.

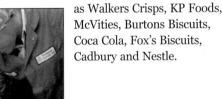

Top: State of the art design at Printpack.
Far left: Maintaining the film rollers. Left: Quality control, Printpack have a determination to settle for nothing less than the highest quality.

Ah - tissue

Each year the top management of a major global enterprise, the Georgia-Pacific Corporation, recognises the dedication to, and improvement in, environmental welfare at its paper mills and awards a 'Chairman's Award for Environmental Excellence' across three categories. In 2003 the winner amongst all the company's European facilities was Bury's own Stubbins Mill.

The selection of Stubbins for the much coveted award was announced at the annual Chairman's Meeting - a conference for the Corporation's Executive Officers and senior managers held in Florida during late February.

The new President European Consumer Products, Bill Schultz, visited the Stubbins Mill on Monday 8th March that year to formally present the award. Accepting it on behalf of the entire Stubbins workforce was Andy Catterall, Site Manger together with Archie Simpson, Stubbins' Technical & Environmental Co-ordinator.

But how on Earth has a firm from Bury become part of a huge multi-national corporation with interests in every part of the globe?

It depends on how far back one wants to go in history. Paper is largely made from sheets of vegetable fibres. The word 'paper' itself comes to us from the ancient Egyptians who made something like paper by gluing together strips of papyrus - a water reed which grew along the banks of the River Nile. That was not of course 'real' paper as we understand it today. The invention of true paper is credited to a chap called Tsai Lun who was China's Minister of Agriculture in 105 AD - though if the present is any guide to the past the more cynical or sceptical might imagine that the true inventor was more likely to have been some unknown and lowly innovator who just happened to work in Tsai Lun's Ministry!

But if China knew all about paper it wasn't about to start exporting the technology to the barbarian lands of the west in a hurry. Europe had to wait for more than a thousand years for paper to make its welcome appearance. Until Marco Polo returned to his native Venice after a tour of the Orient in 1295 paper making was a complete mystery to Europeans. Until then books, then all hand-written, were all produced on parchment, the prepared skins of sheep and goats. It was a very expensive and time consuming process.

Top: From 1969 to 1993 the Mill Manager actually lived on site in this house. Below left: 1992 and the PM3 Machine House takes shape. Below: In the foreground the Effluent Treatment Tower, 1992.

Despite the introduction of paper it was another century or more before full advantage could be taken of the new material. Once John Gutenberg in Germany, and later Thomas Caxton in England, had introduced the printing press the demand for paper began to take off and has never slackened since.

Paper however, was still far from cheap. Sheets of paper were made by hand. Not until the 19th century would methods of industrial production come into their own. By the mid to late 19th century mass production would result for the first time in the possibility of huge print runs of newspapers every day of the week. Such massive production of paper would also result in alternative uses. Where previously paper had been expensive now it was cheap - and yesterdays' newspaper was even cheaper. For the first time people came to think of paper as a disposable commodity: old newspapers famously began to be used for wrapping fish and chips.

And in outhouses across the country cut up sheets of newspapers hanging from a nail provided the poor with a previously unheard of luxury - toilet paper!

For the better off real toilet paper had already made its appearance in the 19th century though wartime shortages in the 20th century would see many who had become accustomed to such luxuries having to revert to 'recycling' as such products became scarce.

Happily in the second half of the 20th century such scarcities would gradually fade in folk's memories, and as shortages disappeared in the same period other new and increasingly affordable paper products crowded for our attention. Who can

Top: A general view of the Mill Manager's house.
Above: PM3's 150 tonne cylinder en route to Stubbins from Beloit, Bolton at Holcombe Brook.

ever forget such innovations as disposable paper underwear and throwaway paper dresses which first made their appearance in the white hot heat of the technology obsessed 1960s? That hard crinkly toilet paper of old has been replaced by soft absorbent multicoloured tissue, whilst the dishcloth of old has been replaced by far more hygienic disposable paper kitchen roll available in colours and patterns which would have been unimaginable to our grandparents. And one of the centres of what has been a world-wide paper revolution has been Bury and its famous Stubbins Mill.

Today the Stubbins Mill employs some 200 people. The paper mill is positioned in the centre of the small village of Stubbins whose population of 3,500 surrounds the mill on three sides.

The mill stands on more than 17 acres of land which once formed part of the Stubbins Estate. The first industrial reference to the site was in 1778 when one Charles Leigh occupied the buildings and used them for calico printing - dyeing on to cotton fabric. From 1778 until 1899 various individuals and companies carried out printing on the site. But for more than a decade after 1900 the mill lay virtually unused until 1911 when it was acquired by James R Crompton Brothers who introduced paper-making for the first time.

Until 1967 the mill would continue to be used for fine paper-making -its products including paper used for products as diverse as cigarettes and bibles.

At the end of the 1960s the Stubbins site was bought by an entrepreneur named Peter Newton who already had several small businesses operating under the Stirling name. As a result of the mill was now renamed Sterling Stubbins.

In 1969 the 'PM1' single-wire tissue machine, 134 inches wide, from Beloit, was installed which became operational in April the following year significantly increasing production.

Another name change occurred in 1971 when Sterling International acquired the company's Horwich

This page: Construction work during the building of PM3.

'converting' site, until then called Mansell Hunt & Catty Ltd; as a result the Horwich site became Sterling Mansell Ltd.

Four years later, in 1975, 'PM2' a 100 inch tissue machine was installed at the Sterling Stubbins mill which became operational in 1976.

The PM2 machine would be rebuilt in 1979 at a cost of £1.5 million to include what was then the latest concept in tissue manufacture: a twin wire former. Together the two machines now in operation would produce some 35,000 tonnes of paper each year.

By the early 1980s Stubbins was experimenting with a mysterious process known as 'deinking' whilst simultaneously developing its Pulp Process Plant One - 'PP1'.

Meanwhile other changes were in the offing. In 1982 the Fort Howard company had bought shares in both Sterling Stubbins and Sterling Mansell. In 1984 Fort Howard acquired full ownership of both sites.

The acquisition by Fort Howard signalled more investment. In the mid-1980s PM1 and PM2 at Stubbins were gradually upgraded at a cost of £5 million, increasing output to some 50,000 tonnes annually. Nor would that be the end of investment: in 1991 work started on PM3 and PP2 at a cost of a remarkable £65 million. That same year more expansion came through the purchase

of Stuart Edgar Ltd based at Bryn in Ashton - in-Makerfield in order to expand the company's converting facilities.

PM3, a five metre wide twin wire tissue machine, became operational in 1993 doubling the mill's output to more than 100,000 tonnes.

Four years after PM3 was commissioned Fort Howard now merged with the James River company to create Fort James, a name which would continue until 2000 when Fort James itself became in turn part of Georgia-Pacific an international business officially known in the United Kingdom as Georgia Pacific GB Ltd. By then Stubbins' flexible operation was producing 100 per cent recycled and 100 per cent virgin products covering the entire product quality range from economy to luxury paper products.

Today Georgia-Pacific and its employees are at the cutting edge of paper-making technology, providing products familiar in households across the whole country. A technology which has its origins in China almost two thousand years ago today has found uses which not only its inventor Tsai Lun, but also Lancashire folk a mere generation or two ago, could not have imagined. In the 21st century, despite the advent of 'paperless office', more paper products are used than ever before - who knows what we'll be using paper for in another two millennia!

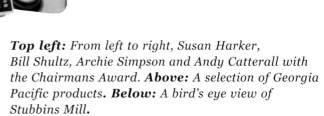

Top left: *From left to right, Susan Harker, Bill Shultz, Archie Simpson and Andy Catterall with the Chairmans Award.* ***Above:*** *A selection of Georgia Pacific products.* ***Below:*** *A bird's eye view of Stubbins Mill.*

The sweetest things

The title of 'That Wicked Shop in Whitefield' undoubtedly goes to that of Slatterys' naughty-but-oh-so-nice patissier and chocolatier. The mouth-watering business that John Slattery and his family have created is the only one of its kind in the country and attracts visitors from far and wide.

The business was founded on 30th June 1967 by Bernard and Margaret Slattery.

Bernard had started his working life as a page boy at the Mayfair cinema before moving on to various other jobs. At 18 Bernard was called up to join the RAF Regiment in which he served in the Middle East desert campaign as a gunner, before spending time in Cairo and later in Italy.

With his hearing damaged Bernard was later put in the cookhouse and bakery. After being demobbed in 1945 he went to work on Manchester liners, baking fresh bread and cakes whilst travelling from Salford Docks to Montreal, each round trip taking a month to complete.

Between trips Bernard went to what was then the Salford technical College to do his formal City & Guilds qualifications in bread and flour confectionery. After qualifying he worked in several bakeries around the area including Bury Co-op and Prestwich Co-op as well as several family businesses all the while gaining experience.

Bernard had married Margaret in 1950; their son John was born in 1953, and daughter Ann in 1959.

*Above: The former 'Masons Arms' building - the new home of Slattery's. **Below:** Founder, Bernard Slattery (centre) in the early days.*

Margaret had done office work since leaving school. In 1939 she had been called up to work in aircraft production at AV Rose in Chadderton. After the war she went to work for CWS in Manchester where she remained until the family began to arrive. But on purchasing the first Slattery business it was back to work for Margaret who took on the running of the shop, and doing the accounts.

The business was a bakery in Cleveland Road, Crumpsall as well as a small shop on Marlborough Road, Higher Broughton, which was supplied each day by the bakery.

It was tough. Bernard and Margaret had borrowed from their family to help buy the business and stock. The first week they had to use all their takings to pay the staff wages. It took quite some time until the business was turning in a profit.

John was 14 when the family went into business; he would help after school and also on a Saturday until he went to Salford College at the age of 16 to formally train for three

years to study baking and confectionery and in the process spending some time in Switzerland.

Sister Ann followed her brother and six years later also went to Salford College. Whilst at College Ann met Stephen Barnes, her husband-to-be, who later also joined the family firm after gaining his own qualifications.

Top: '*He taught me everything I know', John and his father Bernard.* *Left:* *Bernard and Margaret pictured in 1991 as Presidents of Manchester Association of Master Bakers.* *Below:* *A 'pit stop' for the crew of Slattery's whilst on their Lands End to John O' Groats bike ride in aid of the Bakers Benevolent Society.*

The original business was a traditional bakery making everything from scones to wedding cakes. The Slatterys began building a lasting reputation for quality baked products, and for offering good value for money. The business grew both in reputation and size; another shop opened in Salford, replaced in 1979 by one in Prestwich which would remain open until the mid 1980s.

During those years the business won many accolades in national bakery competitions; with John, Ann and Steve taking on all comers to win the UK Bakers of the Year Award four years in a row, defending their title in Birmingham, Manchester and London.

As the bakery flourished so did the family. John married his wife Marilyn, who in due course presented him with daughters Kate and Laura. Ann and Steve had three children: Sarah, Anthony and Joanne.

In 1991 Bernard and Margaret were going to retire, but with growing families to support it was decided that expansion was required. Ann and Steve took over the running of the bakery in Crumpsall, whilst John opened a new business in Whitefield in a rented shop at 156 Bury New Road where he concentrated on the 'Sweet things in Life' producing handmade chocolates, gateaux and desserts alongside birthday, celebration and wedding cakes. And that is when 'That Wicked Shop in Whitefield' was born.

Top left: *Celebrating 21 years business at Crumpsall shop on Cleveland Road.*
Above right: *The family: Anne and Steve, Margaret and Bernard, Marilyn and John, Anthony, Joanne, Sarah, Kate and Laura outside the original shop, 156 Bury New Road in 1990.*
Right: *Anne, John and Steve competing in the UK Bakers Of The Year.*

John's new business took off far faster than expected, and within two years John was looking for larger premises which he found by buying and then extending 190-192 Bury New Road. Later he added number 194 too, when even more space was required.

Despite such growth the core products of the business remain the same today, though with the addition of home-made ice cream, and The Eaterie where delicious home-cooked food can be enjoyed.

An impressive client base has been built up, which includes many well known faces from television and football alongside the many regular visitors looking for a gift with a difference or a celebration cake especially made to take pride of place at a party.

Being less than half a mile from Junction 17 on the M60 makes for easy access to Slattery's from many miles around.

In fact interest in Slattery's comes from even further afield. In 2001 John wrote a book called 'Chocolate Cakes for Weddings and Celebrations' which has sold more than 15,000 copies on the first edition both here and abroad. It has since been reprinted to meet the continuing demand.

A major spin-off from the book would be that people began asking for tuition, in response classes for chocolate skills were started. The classes have become a regular feature of the business, with people even travelling from abroad to take part in Slattery tuition.

tion can be seen. And an open plan 'finishing room' where visitors can actually see Slattery's masterpieces being created.

The new building offers lift access to the first floor, (or stairs for those working off the calories!) and the beautifully appointed 'Masons Dining Room' where music from a grand piano wafts gently through the air creating and the perfect ambience in which to enjoy good food. Walk through this room and there's even a terrace on which to dine al fresco in fine weather.

Alongside the terrace a smart meeting room is available for hire - conferences and presentations being regular uses of this facility, where of course the usual Slattery fine food is available to make business meetings more enjoyable.

Kate, John's eldest daughter worked in the bakery for several years for her Aunty Ann and Uncle Steve whilst she gained her qualifications in baking; she has subsequently joined her father at Whitefield.

Laura, John's youngest daughter went to Nottingham Trent University where she gained a degree in Business Studies before joining the family firm in 2002.

Each Slattery daughter has brought different skills to the business equipping it to move forward.

The original Crumpsall business, now known as Slattery's of Manchester, is under the guidance of Ann and Steve Barnes. A refurbishment programme has extended both the bakery and shop providing a modern environment for their daily production. All the baking is done at Crumpsall, providing John in Whitefield with a constant supply of fresh cake bases, pastry shells etc. for the confectioners and cake decorators to work their magic on.

In 2004 Slattery Patissier & Chocolatier Ltd once again moved to new premises. John and his family bought a local landmark, the former Masons Arms public house, which had been closed and left to fall into disrepair. A full refurbishment of the existing building, first occupied in 1904, took place and a new building built at the rear of the existing one creating a total area of more than 13,000 sq ft.

When one enters this imposing building straight into the sales and showroom area the stunning display of wedding cakes and the sight and aroma of Belgian chocolate attack the senses. The delicious gateaux and desserts - the word 'cakes' is an understatement - offer a genuine feast for the eyes, and are even more satisfying to eat. Celebration cakes of every descrip-

On the second floor can be found the 'Slattery School of Excellence' where course and demonstrations for both the trade and general public are presented, offering a range of food skills covering everything from chocolate, sugar modelling, cake creation and cookery to coffee appreciation and wine tasting.

The Slattery business has been built up by listening to the customer. That old fashioned approach is still the firm's maxim today. What customers want is a high standard of service combined with exceptional quality: and that is what Slattery's consistently provides. Wicked? No, more like wonderful!

Top left: *Winners of the UK Bakers Of The Year 1989 at the new GMEX Exhibition Centre.* ***Above:*** *Examples of stunning cakes created by Slattery's.* ***Below:*** *The new home of Slattery's pictured in 2004.*

Riches from rags

Not many folk can say they've never claimed a single day's sick pay, or never been on the dole. When that boast is made by someone who has worked for more than 70 years the claim is even more remarkable. It's even more extraordinary when one learns that Bury's Lawrence Mortimer began earning his own living at the age of just seven years old!

The company is not only a scrap metal business but also offers a waste container service, haulage and a machinery dismantling service as well as a crane hire business. Most of the processed metal goes to export with a small amount going to steelworks and foundries in the United Kingdom.

Not bad for a firm which was started by a 14 year old boy who left school in 1941 to become a self employed entrepreneur.

In fact Lawrence Mortimer had begun trading on his own account seven years earlier selling firewood from door to door.

Lawrence Mortimer is Bury's scrap metal king. Today his firm, L Mortimer (Bury) Ltd, based in Birch Street, is known around the world.

Top left: *Lawrence Mortimer founder of the company.* **Below:** *L Mortimer (Bury) Ltd's Birch Street premises.*

Lawrence graduated from firewood to selling coal, coke, hot roasted potatoes and ice cream. In those first few years very little was spent on equipment: a hot roasted potato cart and an ice cream cart and a pony and cart cost in total just £70.

After the first three years Lawrence's brother Gerald joined him as partner on equal shares.

Later the brothers started a Marine Store business or rag shop with as many as 16 ponies and horses out making collections each day. By 1960 the firm had had 30-40 employees and had moved from the original premises in Rose Hill off Paradise Street, Bury, to Croft Street where they would remain until 1990 when the present premises in Birch Street were acquired.

Investment in equipment would bring in other kinds of work and help deal with increasing volume of scrap metals. The company bought two new cranes in the early 1960s, one, a four ton 'Iron Fairy' (one of the first hydraulic cranes) and an 8 ton Hydrocon.

Today scrap collections are made from Local authorities, engineering works, building sites and smaller merchants. Deliveries are made directly to the yard by plumbers, builders and small collectors. A waste business operates alongside the scrap business, with much of the work coming from the same customers.

Haulage and crane hire services are provided to engineering businesses, steel erecting companies and builders.

At Birch Street all grades of metal are processed. The company operate the only metal recycling facility in Bury which is registered as exempt from needing a scrap metal yard licence. This is possible only by meeting, and continuing to meet, strict criteria laid down by the Environment Agency, such as having a concreted yard, appropriate drains and an interceptor tank.

The scrap trade is not a particularly glamorous one; and in the 1960s and 70s the firm found it difficult to recruit new staff to meet the volume of work. The Mortimer response was increased investment. Scrap processing has become a highly mechanised business and is now capital rather than labour intensive. Today machines now strip cable, shears cut anything from small copper pipes to thick steel plate, whilst plasma cutters reduce non-ferrous metals to size.

But don't assume that making money from scrap is easy: turnover of scrap is mainly dictated by prices which fluctuate wildly from year to year in a global marketplace. In the last decade prices have fluctuated between £30 and £120 per ton, whilst stainless steel scrap has been priced between £150 and £1,000 per ton!

As for the other side of the business, crane hire and haulage rates have increased steadily over the years but are lower in real terms now than ever before, though inevitably labour, fuel and insurance costs have rocketed upwards

But despite such difficulties L Mortimer Bury Ltd continues to thrive by offering the best service possibly in a friendly personal way and being ready to change and evolve whenever necessary.

The Mortimer tradition is being continued by Lawrence's son David and daughter Jacqueline, but we'll have to wait many more decades yet to discover if they'll beat their father's record for never claiming a day's sick pay!

Top: One of the cranes available for hire from L Mortimer (Bury) Ltd. **Below:** *David Mortimer and Jackie Howarth at the annual dinner of the North Western Metal Association of which David Mortimer was President, 1998.*

Newtons of Bury (est 1900)
The home of beautiful furniture & gifts

The early days

There is a wealth of fascinating history behind the well known quality furnishing business known as Newtons of Bury. The business was founded over a century ago, in the year 1900 by Walter Newton. As trade grew Walter's son, Cyril assisted his father in the firm and set about learning every aspect of the job. As the dark days of the war arrived Cyril joined the Royal Navy and left to serve his country for the duration. The business was originally based in Eccles, and this was its home for many years. Soon after Cyril returned from his war service the decision was taken to move the business to Bury, and a suitable location

was soon found on Spring Street in the town. This served the business well for around 15 years, as the firm built upon its reputation for selling quality second-hand furniture and antiques. By this time Newton's was joined by Colin and Mavis Newton the third generation of the family firm to be involved in the business, it was then decided in 1960 to expand the company to the present site to be known as Newtons Salesrooms.

The business prospered over the next 30 years, despite the ups and downs of the economy and the changing tastes, which characterised this period. In fact whilst most furniture stores were retailing teak and contemporary, which was hugely popular in the 60s and 70s Newton's were doing their own thing i.e. retailing furniture of character, antiques and reproductions. A major milestone was passed in 1992 when the ownership of the business passed into the hands of Glenn and Christine Wild who were not

Above: An illustration of the world famous Moorcroft pottery. Below: An early 20th century photograph looking from the Black Bull to what is now the Newton's store.

from the 1780 and was formerly a private Gentleman's house, to the rear a coach house and stables, with servants quarters in the basement and attic quarters, where only recently a young lady's shoe dating from the early 19th century was uncovered hidden under floor boards. Visitors to the main showrooms of Newtons of Bury cannot fail to be impressed by the unrivalled displays of top quality modern and traditional furniture, which blend beautifully with the fine selection of antiques and collectors' items on offer. The company is the leading stockist's for some of the oldest and most respected furniture manufacturers in the world. The selection of solid English oak furniture attracts buyers from all over England. Smaller collectors' items on show include Moorcroft pottery and lighting, pictures and mirrors, reproduction radios and even world-renowned Steiff classic teddy bears and Winstanly pottery cats.

21st century Changing Tastes

In an ever-changing world, today's furnishings are now sourced from around the globe for character, style and price responding to customer needs. Modern leather upholstery is hugely popular, as are lighter more natural wood shades for cabinet furnishings for bedroom, dining, living and occasional.

Pride

Over the years, generations of the same local families have returned time and again to Newtons of Bury for their furnishing requirements; a source of pride to the current proprietors, Glenn and Christine Wild. The owners have a strong belief in customer loyalty, support for the store and for Bury itself and are working hard to maintain this.

newcomers to the firm, indeed Glenn had already served 30 years with the company, infact, Glenn recalls a particular customer making a purchase with pride knowing that the van would be delivering to her doorstep for the neighbours to see. During that time he learned his trade as a French Polisher and Furniture Restorer. Christine heads the busy manufacturing side of the business, which involves the production of custom-made Table Protectors, 'Wild's Tablecare' which are in great demand from furnishing department stores, and boardrooms for corporate clients throughout the country.

Diversity

By far the most important aspect of the business is still the supply of quality furnishings throughout the north. This is in addition to other services, which include expert furniture restoration, French Polishing and a Re-upholstery service. All these services are carried out by experienced craftsmen in the firm's own workshops which are situated locally and has led to commissioned contracts from all over the north of England.

Georgian House

Deceptive from the outside, many Bury folk and regular customers are aware of the internal size of Newtons store. However, strangers to the town are often amazed by the three storey interior, often describing the store as an 'Aladdin's Cave'. The Georgian building dates

Top right: *A young lady's shoe dating from the early 19th century which was recently uncovered under floor boards at Newton's.* ***Top left and below:*** *Past and present views of the Newton's of Bury store.*

Chemistry lessons

The word 'chemistry' comes to our language from the earlier word 'alchemy', itself derived from 'al-kimia' the Arabic name for Egypt. To Europe's medieval scholars some of the things which Egyptian scientists of a thousand years ago were able to do seemed little short of magic. Today we all share in that magic.

J&W Whewell Ltd's New Bridge Chemical Works in York Street, Radcliffe has been a familiar sight to generations of local residents during the course of more than a century of manufacturing there.

The firm was founded as far back as 1880 by two brothers, Joseph and William Whewell, who specialised in producing resin size and oils. From the outset they employed ten or so people at their New Bridge works premises which they soon extended by incorporating the adjoining Lloyds textile mill.

A second generation of Whewells, also named William and Joseph, (each of the founders named their sons after their own brother) followed on in the business, taking over from their fathers in their turn. Throughout their lives, in addition to their chemical commitments, both of the second generation brothers were fanatically interested in horses. William devoted his life to shire horses and consistently produced show winning specimens from his Heaton Grove stud in Manchester Road. In its heyday the stud had some 30 horses but by 1979 Heaton Grove was sold to a property developer. The old house stood empty

for several years until it was destroyed by fire in 1988.

Long before then however, the management of the business had in turn given way to another

Top left: *Joseph Whewell, co-founder of the company.*
Above: *William Whewell II who at one time had up to 30 shire horses at his Heaton Grove stud.*
Below: *The J&W Whewell haulage fleet, circa 1950s.*

generation - William's daughter Gene and son Joseph Whewell, joined later by the next generation again Joseph III's son William, now took the reins.

Joseph Whewell III started a bulk haulage company operating out of the chemical works. Unhappily the haulage company was not a success and as a result the chemical company was put up for sale. The transport company was bought out by Joseph and his son William and relocated away from the Radcliffe site. J&W Whewell Ltd was now bought by Gene Whewell. The small chemical company was then on the verge of bankruptcy, but with the help of a new accountant Gene was slowly able to turn the business around.

Not that it would be an easy task; progress was at first painfully slow. Lack of investment over many years meant that a major injection of capital was required in the late 1990s, a time which unfortunately coincided with a significant downturn in business. Such problems made life interesting for a couple of difficult years. Happily those problems were eventually to be overcome

Today with some 25 employees the company markets its products in the United Kingdom to many industries, including textiles, lubricants, surfactants formulators, and

the paper and printing trade. Abroad, disinfectant, leather and oils manufacturers are keen to buy from Whewells.

The firm's 400 customers form a very diverse group which includes distributors, and speciality manufacturers. Not being reliant on any one customer has ensured that the company has in recent years not experienced the same highs and lows as other companies.

Astonishingly J&W Whewell Ltd makes over 200 different products which can be categorised into six separate groups: leather chemicals, textile auxiliaries, sulphated chemicals and oils, phosphate esters, sulphosuccinate and soaps. A multi purpose plant allows the company to manufacture all these different types of chemicals on site.

The company really is a specialist one: the firm is one of only two manufacturers of sulphated oils and chemicals in the United Kingdom. Best of all from a customer's point of view is that being multi-skilled and of a modest size the company is flexible enough to offer them unique solutions - tailor made products for their specific needs.

Following triumph and near disaster, followed by triumph yet again, today's Whewell-in-charge of the family firm, still Gene Whewell, intends to redevelop the historic site, which as served her family so well over the passing decades. She intends to soon remove the old 'sulphation' building and warehouse adjacent to the river.

Top left: Mr & Mrs William Whewell II.
Below: Gene Whewell pictured outside the company's New Bridge Chemical Works.

Excelling in Bury

Today one of the best known names on Bury's industrial scene is the Excelsior Group, based at Hartshead Works in Deal Street.

Excelsior Limited traces its origins back to a company originally established in 1896 by two Swiss businessmen. Today's Excelsior Group is very much a family business; started by Kenneth Fielding it is now run by John Fielding, currently Chairman and Managing Director; Giles Fielding is Sales and Marketing Director whilst Karen Fielding, Giles' wife is Group Accountant.

In 1902 when Excelsior became a limited company it specialised in the manufacture of vulcanised fibre containers, mainly supplying the textile industry, but also making storage boxes and briefcases sold under the 'Neverdone' brand name.

The company moved to Ferngrove Mills off Rochdale Old Road in 1946 after a disastrous fire destroyed its original premises in Bacup.

In 1952 the company was bought by the Fielding family, industrialists from Rochdale. The Fieldings continued to build on the reputation of the Neverdone brand range. In the 1970s however, the decline in the textile industry signalled the need for a change in emphasis and a switch was made to rotational moulding, using plastics to make trucks sold to dyehouses and laundries.

Since the beginning of the 1980s the company has expanded dramatically and made several acquisitions. In 1990 this resulted in the formation of Excelsior Group International Ltd which was established in order to provide resources to its several subsidiaries.

Following these changes there are now two operating companies in the Excelsior Group: Excelsior Limited and Crossfield Excalibur Limited.

Excelsior developed its first rotationally moulded plastic trucks in the 1970s under the name of Excelsior Containers Ltd. The company changed its name to Excelsior Rotational Moulding Ltd in 1994.

ERM produces a vast range of materials-handling products. It is involved with various industries including the industrial mail order, automotive, sport and leisure and construction sectors, and deals with several blue chip companies such as MG Rover, JCB, Hepworths, Argos and Grattan. ERM have become increasingly involved in the exhibition/display industry, specialising in the manufacture of cases for transporting and protecting exhibition equipment.

Above: A Neverdone brochure cover from the early 1940s.

substantial experience in the manufacture of equipment for the display and exhibition industries.

Crossfield Excalibur Ltd was established in October 1998 as the result of the merger of Crossfield Patterns Ltd of Rochdale with Excalibur Metal Products Ltd.

CEL specialises in the manufacture of sheet steel and cast aluminium tooling for the rotational moulding and vacuum forming industries. Over the years this has been greatly assisted by continued investment in the latest CAD technology.

In October 2002, Excelsior Case and Container Ltd, based at Irwell Works and Excelsior Rotational Moulding Limited based at Hartshead Works were formally integrated to create a new company, Excelsior Ltd. The main purpose of

In a growing industry ERM has established itself as one of Europe's market leaders with a quarter of its sales going abroad.

In October 2000 Smith Rotational Moulding Ltd, already part of the Group, was merged with ERM to create a single rotational moulder with a much larger product portfolio.

Excelsior Case and Container Ltd was formed in 1994 from Excelsior Containers Ltd. This was established as a specialist unit dealing with the design and manufacture of a wide range of products for the transportation and protection of goods in sectors ranging from aeronautics to entertainment.

ECC uses many different types of material such as extruded plastic sheet, aluminium and PVC-coated plywood, fluted plastic sheet and fibreboard. It produces a large range of standard products but also has the ability to manufacture to almost any specification. ECC is also a vacuum forming specialist, a manufacturer of nylon carry bag systems, and also has

this was to make life easier for customers who would only have to deal with one account in future. Sales and all financial operations for both sites have been amalgamated and moved to Head Office at Hartshead Works, though production continues to be done at two separate sites

Today, with over 120 employees, the Excelsior Group has an annual turnover of more than £6 million - not a bad package!

Top left: *Excelsior's Irwell Works.*
Left: *John Fielding, Chairman and Managing Director (seated) and Giles Fielding, Sales and Marketing Director.*

Let's talk rubbish

Since 1960 the arrival of smokeless zones meant that burning rubbish was no longer the easy option it had once been. Demand for specialist waste disposal firms inevitably increased. One of those was the now familiar name of Wheeldon Brothers Waste Ltd.

Brothers John Bagshaw Wheeldon and Luke Bagshaw Wheeldon first established their business in 1965. Since its incorporation in 1976 the business has flourished. The company is now being managed by a second generation of the Wheeldon family helped by some two dozen staff who run twenty radio-controlled wagons throughout Greater Manchester.

Before starting their waste disposal business the Wheeldon brothers worked as labourers on their parents', John Henry Bagshaw Wheeldon and Gladys Wheeldon's farm, Ryecroft Farm, Rochdale Road East, Heywood. At the farm the brothers helped their father and mother raise pigs and a few cows, as well as operating a milk round.

From an early age John and Luke's parents instilled hard work as a top priority. This ethic helped them both see that through dedication to customers their goals could be achieved, which was to improve the environment and help the business grow.

The waste business began when John B Wheeldon bought a wagon for collecting food waste for the pigs, and also, started occasionally collecting other waste. Gradually farming was reduced as the demand for waste collection increased.

For 20 years John and Luke ran the business from Ryecroft Farm helped by their wives Glenda and Patricia. In 1984 however, the brothers took a major step forward when they bought a waste transfer station in Mossdown Road, Oldham.

Top: *John and Luke Wheeldon take a drive on the farm, 1950s.* ***Below:*** *John (middle) and Luke (right) working as labourers on their parents farm, also pictured is their cousin Frank (left).*

Patricia understandably , deciding to no longer be involved in the business. They both continue to be missed, at the company and personally.

Today John and Glenda helped by their children, Susan, Jonathan and James, now run the company. John and James are mechanics, Glenda deals with skip hire and with customers and drivers. Susan is the accountant, whilst Jonathan is transfer station manager in Oldham.

Wheeldon Brothers Waste Ltd offers its services to all kinds of clients, though its main customers come from manufacturing, packaging and transport companies, restaurants, shops, builders, construction alongside some 'domestic' work.

Growth has been achieved by providing a reliable , fast and effective service beyond clients' expectations. For the future the firm aims to grow even larger, not least with eco-friendly plans to produce a product from re-cycled shredded tyres.

The company's mission is continue to strive for a cleaner environment, to assist customers to dispose of their waste correctly and to continue to meet the needs of their customers.

The business has come a long way from that first wagon bought for picking up food waste for pigs.

In 1991 they also acquired a unit on the Yeargate Industrial Estate at Heap Bridge, Bury.

Over the passing years, from that first wagon bought for collecting food waste, the business would gradually expand its range of services. That expansion started with skips, at first 8 cubic yard skips; then 'rolonof' 20-40 cubic yard skips, then 'REL' 14 cubic yard skips, before moving into compactor wagons and finally wheelie bins.

The growth of the business would be helped immeasurably by successive governments' 'green' legislation, such as land fill tax, intended to control the disposal of waste. The Wheeldons would take full advantage of the opportunities presented to them by obtaining licenses for disposing of special wastes such as asbestos, oils and tyres.

But building a business is not all plain sailing. In 1996 a large fire broke out at Heap Bridge. In the conflagration not only the building but also wagons, business records, electric installations, telephones and machinery were destroyed. Happily, with everyone working together, the firm somehow managed to continue with little disruption to customers. Indeed the fire was the spur to even more growth: the Heap Bridge site would be expanded by the purchase of an additional unit in 1998.

Sadly co-founder Luke Wheeldon passed away in 1999; that major loss to the company was compounded by Luke's widow

Top left: An early Wheeldon wagon.
Above left: One of the company's Heil Big Bite vehicles used to service the Greater Manchester area.
Below: The current management at Wheeldon Brothers Waste Ltd, from left to right:
James Wheeldon, Glenda Wheeldon, John Wheeldon, Susan Ward and Jonathan Wheeldon.

Ernest Platt (Bury) Ltd
The seal of approval

One of Bury's best known firms is 'Ernie Platts' - Ernest Platt (Bury) Ltd to give the company its Sunday best title. Today the firm is a major supplier of rubber materials, gaskets, seals, extrusions, plastics, packings, hoses, fittings and thermal insulation products to the engineering industry.

The firm was established in the mid 19th century as a rubber merchants and mill furnishers. William A Platt started his humble business from his family home in Walmersley Road under the name of WA Platt & Son. William's expertise in his field soon earned him the nickname India Rubber Bill.

Before long William began to expand and diversify the business, moving into boiler, pipe and heat insulation. Recognising an enormous market he devised and manufactured his own insulation compounds in the works in Buckley Street behind his home. As all local factories and mills at that time were steam powered this was a boom time for Platt's products.

In the late 1890s until the first world war almost all ships in the Royal Navy's fleet

Top: *William Platt, son of the founder.*
Below: *A 1908 company letterhead.*
Right: *Insulation work at East Lancashire Paper Mill, 1955.*

were also steam powered. WA Platt & Son gained a lucrative and highly sought after Admiralty contract to design and install the boiler pipes and heating in the fleet.

The 'son' in WA Platt & Son, also called William, was a councillor, JP and local church dignitary. A highly intelligent man he helped with the War Savings Movement and was also heavily involved with the Friendly Societies Movement. He was consulted by the Government, being an acknowledged authority on National Health Insurance and Old Age Pensions. He helped to set up Lloyd George's famous National Insurance Bill of 1911 and later locally implemented the National Health Insurance Act. For his work in this field he was awarded the MBE in 1912, and in 1932 the OBE.

Inevitably, because of all his Governmental work, William Platt junior could not spend as much time on his company as he would have liked. Consequently WA Platt & Son suffered, leading to 'downsizing' during the

steady expansion around gasket manufacture and sealing material technology with the company now supplying a vast range of products, not least bespoke fabrication of special insulation and thermal materials for use anywhere where heat loss or expansion and contraction due to heat variations are a problem.

Not surprisingly the power industry is a major customer, but the company has also done much to help the tunnelling industry, such as providing large (nine metre diameter) entry/exit seals for the Channel Tunnel Rail Link as well as inflatable seals to stop land subsidence on large sewerage outlets.

Now with Stephen Platt still firmly at the helm 'Ernie Platts' supplies major national companies in engineering, metal fabrication, boiler maintenance, heating and ventilation, the power industry and civil engineering. Understandably the company prides itself on the fact that it offers a first class service, a service honed to perfection by more than a century and a half of experience.

Depression, although the company continued to trade steadily throughout those years, doing much the same work as before.

William Platt died in 1933, leaving the business in the hands of his son Ernest Alexander Platt. The business continued in much the same way throughout the 1940s and 1950s, still doing many contractual insulation jobs in the late 1950s.

When Ernest Platt died in 1951; his son Wilfred now formed a limited company named after his father - today's Ernest Platt (Bury) Ltd. Over the next two decades Wilfred instituted a process of further diversification, moving away from mill furnishings and boiler insulation in a period when many local mills were slowly dying.

Wilfred Platt moved the company's focus more towards the field of gasket manufacture and sealing materials. This proved enormously successful.

In 1972 Wilfred's son Stephen joined the company and by 1978 Wilfred had left control of the business to his son, the fifth generation of the Platt family. During the recession of the 1980s which led to the decline and the closure of many local factories and engineering works Stephen saw the need for expansion to broaden both the company's outlook and customer base: with this in mind the company opened a branch in Blackburn in 1983.

Steady trading has continued ever since with 1990 seeing the company moving for the very first time - to its present site the Greenacre Works off Whalley Road, Shuttleworth, Ramsbottom. The move brought the whole operation under one roof. Since then there has been a

Top: *Testing of an inflatable seal.*
Below (both pictures): *At approximately 9m in*

diameter this Entry Seal (left)was produced by Ernest Platt (Bury) Ltd for use with tunnelling machines on the Channel Tunnel Rail Link as can be seen below.

The home front

One of the country's best known housing charities is the Abbeyfield Society. It was in 1956 that Richard Carr-Gomm founded the Society as an expression of Christian concern for the elderly; he wanted to relieve the loneliness he found amongst older people living in the East End of London.

Today there are 500 local Abbeyfield Societies affiliated to the national body, between them running some 800 homes.

In 1961 Richard wrote to all the Mayors in England asking them if they would start up an Abbeyfield House. The Mayor of Bury was Alderman Peter Manners who decided to make that his project for his year in office. In 1962 the Mayor called a public meeting held in the Derby Hall, Market Street, at which an Executive Committee was elected.

The Executive Committee soon purchased 167 Spring Street on the corner of Heywood Street for £1,150, the money being borrowed from Bury Corporation. Another £600 was borrowed for refurbishment. The house consisted of a small lounge/dining room, five residents' rooms, one bathroom and two rooms in the attic for a housekeeper.

In 1964 the Society bought a house in Thrush Drive known as Chesham Bank for £3,600 again with a loan from Bury Corporation. After refurbishment this provided accommodation for up to 11 residents with a kitchen, a dining room, a lounge and two bathrooms.

The committee decided to erect a purpose-built house in 1972, and with the help of the Rotary Club of Bury built Abbeyfield House at 406 Bolton Road. The new building contained seven residents' rooms, two bathrooms, two WCs, a kitchen, lounge/dining room and housekeeper's accommodation. The cost of the land was £2,000 and the cost of building some £20,000.

The Society's first Chairman, former Mayor Peter Manners, died in 1982, and after 20 years as Hon. Secretary Jack Farraday took on the office of Chairman.

In 1984 the Committee again decided to look for land for another purpose-built home to replace Chesham Bank which required a lot of money spending on it. A plot of land at 68/78 Tottington Road was found.

After a year's negotiation a grant of 95 per cent was obtained from the Housing Corporation towards the cost

Above: Jack Farraday (left), co-founder of Abbeyfield Bury Society and the Society's first Chairman Alderman Peter Manners. Below left: Abbeyfield Society, Manchester Road. Below: The opening of Templeton House in 1988. Today's Chairman Mr Maurice Birch and Hon. Secretary Mrs Mavis Rothwell can be seen second from the left and extreme left.

of building. Late in 1984 a Mrs Templeton bequeathed the sum of £185,000 to the Society.

The money was soon being put to good use: in 1985 the Holy Cross College decided to sell its Sixth Form College buildings in Manchester Road which the Society now bought for £30,000.

Work began on the Tottington Road and Manchester Road sites in December 1986. Both projects were completed exactly one year later at a cost of £230,000 each. After moving the residents from Chesham Bank to Manchester Road the former building was sold for £68,000, which together with Mrs Templeton's legacy paid for the Manchester Road house.

In 1989 the Whitefield Abbeyfield Society was losing money and had only three members left on its Executive Committee: they approached the Bury Society with an offer to merge. At the time of the merger it was agreed that the Whitefield Home required too much money spending on it and that there were too many floors: it was agreed by both Societies that the solution was to sell the building and transfer the two remaining residents to the Bury Homes.

In 1992 the Government and Housing Corporation required better accommodation for sheltered housing and so the Committee again applied to the Housing Corporation for a grant to up-grade the Tottington Road house, making all rooms en-suite. The Housing Corporation offered a grant of £228,000 and work began on a project to refurbish and extend the building at a cost of £650,000 providing 14 en-suite bedrooms which were completed in December 2001.

The committee applied to the Housing Corporation for a grant to refurbish the Manchester Road house in October 2001 to provide similar en-suite accommodation. Work began on that project in August 2002, providing 10 en-suite residents' rooms and additional Housekeeper accommodation at a total cost of £540,000.

In 2002 the Radcliffe Abbeyfield Society was having difficulties in attracting volunteers and sought help from the Bury Society. Another merger was agreed with the Chairman and Secretary of the Radcliffe Society joining the Bury Committee, now managed from the Bury Abbeyfield office at Farraday House in Tottington Road.

The Bury Abbeyfield Society Ltd remains a non-profit making company registered as a charity which is always pleased to welcome new volunteers.

Top left: An interior view of Abbeyfield's Manchester Road home. Below: Faraday House, Tottington Road. Bottom: Residents and guests enjoy a brass band musical evening in the grounds of Tottington Road, June 2003.

Tick tock at the rock

Number 26 The Rock in Bury is home to one of the town's oldest retail establishments. There one can find some of the finest watches and jewellery in Bury at the firm of Lepp's Ltd.

For a century now Bury folk have been buying their watches and jewellery at Lepp's shop. Many of those watches are now treasured family heirlooms. By comparison to many of today's cheap throwaway digital watches the timepieces of yesteryear were, and indeed still are, valuable and valued works of art. Can you remember sitting on your grandfather's knee when he pulled out his gold hunter from his waistcoat pocket? How many of us share such a memory? How many of us recall the days when a gentlemen's pride and joy was his pocket watch on a golden chain, perhaps with a half sovereign or masonic seal attached, not only something with which to tell the time but an object to be admired as a thing of beauty as well as being a delightful status symbol.

How many small children have been amused by a doting grandfather who sat them on his lap and let them listen to the mysterious tick-tock emanating from inside the shiny golden case of his watch? Sadly these days few youngsters will enjoy such small pleasures and grow up to recall such fond memories - digital watches simply don't have a tick, nor come to that a tock either.

But knowing the in and outs of both ticks and tocks has been the lifeblood of Lepp's Ltd and the Lepp family for more than a hundred years.

Above: Founder, James Ditchfield Lepp in 1928 in his term as Mayor of Bury. Below: JD Lepp's original shop can be seen second from the right (between the Union Jack and the Tobacconist) in this early 20th century picture.

diamond and gem set jewellery, as well as a specialist range of second-hand jewellery.

As Bury's oldest established privately owned jeweller the business prides itself on its personal service, attention to detail and 'Olde Worlde' courtesy which is so often lacking in today's impersonal retail world.

The business has five staff managed by Miss B Halliwell assisted by Mrs S Howard. Lepp's also offers a valuation service for insurance and probate carried out by Mr G Fielding. Mr Fielding, a Director of the company, is the possessor of not only the Professional Jeweller's Diploma and its Valuation Diploma but is also a Fellow of the National Association of Goldsmiths and a member of the Diamond Gem Association.

The present business was founded by local man, James Ditchfield Lepp, in 1905 when he opened the shop under his name as a jewellers and watchmakers. Mr Lepp was a fully trained watchmaker and jeweller and had earlier in his career left Bury, but at the age of 35 he returned to the town to buy the business of what had until then been Waldvogel & Co. a company which had first been established in a shop opposite St John's Church in 1836.

At the time James Lepp returned to Bury the business was mainly supported by the repair trade. As time passed however, the jewellery side of the business began to flourish and James Lepp became an established figure in the local community, becoming president of the Bury Tradesmen's Association and Treasurer of the Manchester and District Federation of Chambers of Trade. In 1928 James Lepp became Mayor of Bury being notable during his term of office for promoting the War Memorial and the extension of the Children's Ward at the Bury General Hospital.

In the early 1930s the founder was obliged to move to warmer climes for health reasons and in 1935 he opened a jewellery business in Newquay Cornwall. Lepp's of Bury however, now a limited company, continued as a managed business until James Lepp's death in 1957 at which time the business passed to his son John Lepp, who, with his wife Antonia, still owns the company.

The Lepp family also own two other jewellery businesses, one in Altrincham and one on Warrington.

Lepp's of Bury is fortunate to have the sole Rolex watch concession for the town, though the firm also carries a wide range of other watch brands in addition to a large range of Italian and British made gold,

Founded in the Edwardian era when real clockwork was the only way that watches could be made to run, the firm of Lepp's Ltd has seen major changes in the business of timekeeping: the speaking clock, the atomic clock and the first primitive Sinclair digital watch. But happily some things never change: skill, craftsmanship

and quality are surely virtues which, like diamonds, last forever.

Top left: *Manageress Beverley Halliwel and Assistant Manageress Shirley Howard.*
Left: *Mr John Lepp and Mrs Antonia Lepp.*
Below: *Lepps Ltd, 26 The Rock, 2004*

The sky's the limit for
Radcliffe Glass & Windows Ltd

These days it seems everyone wants double-glazed windows and a conservatory in their homes. One of the first local firms to offer double-glazing was Radcliffe Glass & Windows Ltd.

Radcliffe Glass was established in Mellor Street, Radcliffe in 1979 by local joiner Peter Andrew Turner and his wife Iris, after an earlier venture into joinery in partnership with Peter's brother had failed to work out.

The firm began by doing simple glazing work and cutting glass to size. In 1985 however, Radcliffe Glass became the first double-glazing unit manufacturer in the area. With little competition the business flourished.

In 1987 Steven Ainsworth started work at Radcliffe Glass straight from school, helping make double glazing units. After a brief period working in the factory Steven was taught how to glaze, cut, polish, edge, lead and drill all types of glass.

By then there were three members of staff, including Steven, working in an increasingly busy business.

In 1992 the firm moved to Lodge Brow to make way for new roads which were then being built in Radcliffe. After the move there were fewer employees as the once-thriving business found itself against some major competition.

With the business having reached its peak in the late 1980s Radcliffe Glass appeared to have seen its best years.

As the business slowed down only Steven Ainsworth was left of the original team. Often Steven found himself on his own running the business with Peter Turner dropping in only occasionally.

In 1999 Peter asked Steven if he was interested in buying the firm as he was now ready for retirement. Steven and his wife Susan discussed the offer for some time. Susan also mentioned the offer to her brother Clive Powers.

New lines were introduced such as 'Rosewood' a superior wood-effect PVC. But with competition in the UPVC window replacement field getting harder Radcliffe Glass & Windows now branched out into the conservatory market. In the second year turnover again increased by more than 200 per cent.

The third year of trading began with not only an increasing volume of installations but also with commissions from high profile customers such as Bolholt Country Park Hotel, Polyflor, Harwood Golf Club and Bury Grammar School for Girls.

Turnover was now becoming so large that the partners' accountant advised them that that the business should become a limited company.

From running one van the company now purchased two new ones fitted with the latest specification in racks for transporting glass. Another window installer was employed to provide two installation teams, whilst an office manager had to be taken on to help Clive with his administrative tasks.

At Lodge Brow major changes were made to the premises, opening up the rear of the building to provide a showroom and office as well as a trade counter.

Yet again an increase of more than 200 per cent was to be recorded over the next 12 months.

In 2004 the firm celebrated 25 years in the glass business. It was indeed an occasion to celebrate, not least in that Steven and Clive had seen annual turnover reach a staggering £1 million. And with the bulk of new sales coming from customer recommendations the future now looks clear for Radcliffe Glass & Windows Ltd.

Before long Steven and Clive were discussing the possibility of a partnership.

In February 2001 Steven Ainsworth and his brother in law Clive Powers became the new owners of Radcliffe Glass - though altering the name to Radcliffe Glass and Windows to mark their wider ambitions.

Clive had come from a sales and marketing background working for larger companies such as the Bank of Scotland and General Electric. Clive's knowledge of marketing and administration coupled with Steven's wealth of experience of glass and glazing soon began to impact on the business.

Within three weeks 'Fair Trades' membership had been applied for. Within six months cutting-edge glass-processing machinery had been bought, as well as higher specification window frames introduced. A computer was also acquired.

More UPVC window and door installations were made, despite stiff competition, whilst some of the larger kitchen and bathroom companies began to use the firm again. Clive's wife, Kelly-Marie, who did all of the book-keeping during the first 18 months, soon found herself with plenty to keep count of.

In the first year turnover increased by more than 200 per cent, and an extra glass cutter had to be taken on.

In the second year another window fitter was employed to help with larger installations.

Left: An aerial view of Radcliffe Glass, Circa 1970s.
Top: Early Radcliffe Glass advertising.
Right: Owners of Radcliffe Glass & Windows, Steven Ainsworth (left) and Clive Powers

Acknowledgments

The publishers would like to thank

Bury Archive Service

Andrew Mitchell

Steve Ainsworth

True North Books Ltd - Book List

Memories of Accrington - 1 903204 05 4

Memories of Barnet - 1 903204 16 X

Memories of Barnsley - 1 900463 11 3

More Memories of Barnsley - 1 903 204 79 8

Golden Years of Barnsley -1 900463 87 3

Memories of Basingstoke - 1 903204 26 7

Memories of Bedford - 1 900463 83 0

More Memories of Bedford - 1 903204 33 X

Golden Years of Birmingham - 1 900463 04 0

Birmingham Memories - 1 903204 45 3

Memories of Blackburn - 1 900463 40 7

More Memories of Blackburn - 1 900463 96 2

Memories of Blackpool - 1 900463 21 0

Memories of Bolton - 1 900463 45 8

More Memories of Bolton - 1 900463 13 X

Bolton Memories - 1 903204 37 2

Memories of Bournemouth -1 900463 44 X

Memories of Bradford - 1 900463 00 8

More Memories of Bradford - 1 900463 16 4

More Memories of Bradford II - 1 900463 63 6

Bradford Memories - 1 903204 47 X

Bradford City Memories - 1 900463 57 1

Memories of Bristol - 1 900463 78 4

More Memories of Bristol - 1 903204 43 7

Memories of Bromley - 1 903204 21 6

Memories of Burnley - 1 900463 95 4

Golden Years of Burnley - 1 900463 67 9

Memories of Bury - 1 900463 90 3

Memories of Cambridge - 1 900463 88 1

Memories of Cardiff - 1 900463 14 8

More Memories of Cardiff - 1 903204 73 9

Memories of Carlisle - 1 900463 38 5

Memories of Chelmsford - 1 903204 29 1

Memories of Cheltenham - 1 903204 17 8

Memories of Chester - 1 900463 46 6

More Memories of Chester -1 903204 02 X

Memories of Chesterfield -1 900463 61 X

More Memories of Chesterfield - 1 903204 28 3

Memories of Colchester - 1 900463 74 1

Nostalgic Coventry - 1 900463 58 X

Coventry Memories - 1 903204 38 0

Memories of Croydon - 1 900463 19 9

More Memories of Croydon - 1 903204 35 6

Golden Years of Darlington - 1 900463 72 5

Nostalgic Darlington - 1 900463 31 8

Darlington Memories - 1 903204 46 1

Memories of Derby - 1 900463 37 7

More Memories of Derby - 1 903204 20 8

Memories of Dewsbury & Batley - 1 900463 80 6

Memories of Doncaster - 1 900463 36 9

More Memories of Doncaster - 1 903204 75 5

Nostalgic Dudley - 1 900463 03 2

Golden Years of Dudley - 1 903204 60 7

Memories of Edinburgh - 1 900463 33 4

More memories of Edinburgh - 1903204 72 0

Memories of Enfield - 1 903204 14 3

Memories of Exeter - 1 900463 94 6

Memories of Glasgow - 1 900463 68 7

More Memories of Glasgow - 1 903204 44 5

Memories of Gloucester - 1 903204 04 6

Memories of Grimsby - 1 900463 97 0

More Memories of Grimsby - 1 903204 36 4

Memories of Guildford - 1 903204 22 4

Memories of Halifax - 1 900463 05 9

More Memories of Halifax - 1 900463 06 7

Golden Years of Halifax - 1 900463 62 8

Nostalgic Halifax - 1 903204 30 5

Memories of Harrogate - 1 903204 01 1

Memories of Hartlepool - 1 900463 42 3

Memories of High Wycombe - 1 900463 84 9

Memories of Huddersfield - 1 900463 15 6

More Memories of Huddersfield - 1 900463 26 1

Golden Years of Huddersfield - 1 900463 77 6

Nostalgic Huddersfield - 1 903204 19 4

Huddersfield Town FC - 1 900463 51 2

Memories of Hull - 1 900463 86 5

More Memories of Hull - 1 903204 06 2

Hull Memories - 1 903204 70 4

Memories of Ipswich - 1 900463 09 1

More Memories of Ipswich - 1 903204 52 6

Memories of Keighley - 1 900463 01 6

True North Books Ltd - Book List

Memories of Kingston - 1 903204 24 0

Memories of Leeds - 1 900463 75 X

More Memories of Leeds - 1 900463 12 1

Golden Years of Leeds - 1 903204 07 0

Memories of Leicester - 1 900463 08 3

Leeds Memories - 1 903204 62 3

More Memories of Leicester - 1 903204 08 9

Memories of Leigh - 1 903204 27 5

Memories of Lincoln - 1 900463 43 1

Memories of Liverpool - 1 900463 07 5

More Memories of Liverpool - 1 903204 09 7

Liverpool Memories - 1 903204 53 4

Memories of Luton - 1 900463 93 8

Memories of Macclesfield - 1 900463 28 8

Memories of Manchester - 1 900463 27 X

More Memories of Manchester - 1 903204 03 8

Manchester Memories - 1 903204 54 2

Memories of Middlesbrough - 1 900463 56 3

More Memories of Middlesbrough - 1 903204 42 9

Memories of Newbury - 1 900463 79 2

Memories of Newcastle - 1 900463 81 4

More Memories of Newcastle - 1 903204 10 0

Newcastle Memories - 1.903204 71 2

Memories of Newport - 1 900463 59 8

Memories of Northampton - 1 900463 48 2

More Memories of Northampton - 1 903204 34 8

Memories of Norwich - 1 900463 73 3

Memories of Nottingham - 1 900463 91 1

More Memories of Nottingham - 1 903204 11 9

Nottingham Memories - 1 903204 63 1

Bygone Oldham - 1 900463 25 3

Memories of Oldham - 1 900463 76 8

Memories of Oxford - 1 900463 54 7

Memories of Peterborough - 1 900463 98 9

Golden Years of Poole - 1 900463 69 5

Memories of Portsmouth - 1 900463 39 3

More Memories of Portsmouth - 1 903204 51 8

Nostalgic Preston - 1 900463 50 4

More Memories of Preston - 1 900463 17 2

Preston Memories - 1 903204 41 0

Memories of Reading - 1 900463 49 0

Memories of Rochdale - 1 900463 60 1

More Memories of Reading - 1 903204 39 9

More Memories of Rochdale - 1 900463 22 9

Memories of Romford - 1 903204 40 2

Memories of Rotherham - 1 903 204 77 1

Memories of St Albans - 1 903204 23 2

Memories of St Helens - 1 900463 52 0

Memories of Sheffield - 1 900463 20 2

More Memories of Sheffield - 1 900463 32 6

Golden Years of Sheffield - 1 903204 13 5

Memories of Slough - 1 900 463 29 6

Golden Years of Solihull - 1 903204 55 0

Memories of Southampton - 1 900463 34 2

More Memories of Southampton - 1 903204 49 6

Memories of Stockport - 1 900463 55 5

More Memories of Stockport - 1 903204 18 6

Memories of Stockton - 1 900463 41 5

Memories of Stoke-on-Trent - 1 900463 47 4

More Memories of Stoke-on-Trent - 1 903204 12 7

Memories of Stourbridge - 1903204 31 3

Memories of Sunderland - 1 900463 71 7

More Memories of Sunderland - 1 903204 48 8

Memories of Swindon - 1 903204 00 3

Memories of Uxbridge - 1 900463 64 4

Memories of Wakefield - 1 900463 65 2

More Memories of Wakefield - 1 900463 89 X

Nostalgic Walsall - 1 900463 18 0

Golden Years of Walsall - 1 903204 56 9

More Memories of Warrington - 1 900463 02 4

Memories of Watford - 1 900463 24 5

Golden Years of West Bromwich - 1 900463 99 7

Memories of Wigan - 1 900463 85 7

Golden Years of Wigan - 1 900463 82 2

Nostalgic Wirral - 1 903204 15 1

Wirral Memories - 1 903204 74 7

Memories of Woking - 1 903204 32 1

Nostalgic Wolverhampton - 1 900463 53 9

Wolverhampton Memories - 1 903204 50 X

Memories of Worcester - 1 903204 25 9

Memories of Wrexham - 1 900463 23 7

Memories of York - 1 900463 66 0

Available in the Local Interest section of all major bookshops or direct from the publishers - telephone 01422 344344